6| 01

- 6 JAN 2012

The Life and Loves of
Barbara
STANWYCK

Books by Jane Ellen Wayne include:

The Life of Robert Taylor
Gable's Women
Stanwyck
Crawford's Men
Gary Cooper
Clark Gable: Portrait of a Misfit
Ava's Men
The Life and Loves of Grace Kelly
The Golden Girls of MGM
The Leading Men of MGM

The Life and Loves of

Barbara
STANWYCK

Jane Ellen Wayne

BOOKS

First published in Great Britain in 2009 by
JR Books, 10 Greenland Street, London NW1 0ND
www.jrbooks.com

A catalogue record for this book is available from the British Library.

ISBN 978-1-906217-94-5

1 3 5 7 9 10 8 6 4 2

Printed by MPG Books, Bodmin, Cornwall

Contents

To Miss Ellie

Introduction

In 1969 I began writing the biography of Barbara Stanwyck's second husband, handsome actor Robert Taylor, who had recently died.

She was reluctant to talk to me about him, but suggested I call her secretary when I arrived in Los Angeles. To my surprise and delight, she agreed to an interview, but an hour before we were scheduled to meet she cancelled our appointment. My admiration for Stanwyck prevented me from dropping her a note about how the scales were tipped in Taylor's favour because I could find no one who had a kind word to say about her other than professionally.

John Wayne suggested, 'Barbara was either drunk when she agreed to see you or drunk when she backed out. Bob was her only weakness. I'm told she built a shrine to him in her house and probably won't see you because she can't bear to talk about him. She threatened to bleed him for the rest of his life if he went through with the divorce. He did and she did.'

Joan Crawford, who was one of Stanwyck's closest friends,

told me basically the same thing. They had been great friends since their hoofer days during the roaring twenties in New York City where they hung out in lesbian bars and had too many abortions that later prevented them from having children.

'Barbara was nominated for an Oscar four times and never won,' Crawford explained. 'She deserved an award, but I don't think she was popular with her peers because she didn't socialise much and refused to play up to people. Her first husband was the conceited comic Frank Fay who was always fighting with someone including Barbara. They adopted a baby and he threw it in the swimming pool! Then she married Bob Taylor and sent the kid away to school. She was not meant to be a mother. When he joined the army she shook the kid's hand and that was it. I don't think she ever saw him again.'

Both Crawford and Stanwyck had humble beginnings. Their lack of education and family life put them on the street to fend for themselves. They clawed their way to the top, drank and smoked too much, had too many frivolous affairs and married the wrong men. Joan said she had no regrets, but Barbara had one, and she proved it on 11 June 1969, a warm Wednesday in Glendale, California.

An organ chimed 'Some Enchanted Evening,' romantic, sentimental and touching, but people were not dancing or singing. They were paying their respects. In Forest Lawn's tiny Church of the Recessional a beautiful German-born widow entered the vestibule with her two children, both fair and blond in contrast to their parents.

As the familiar tune 'I'll Get By' echoed through the Rudyard Kipling Gardens that hugged the stone chapel, the silver-haired Stanwyck made her slow and pitiful entrance held up by two men. She wore yellow because the man she loved once told her not to wear black to his funeral. All eyes were on her that day, a rarity in Hollywood where everyone had seen it all. Those few minutes were irritating to many, pathetic to some and shocking to all. Although she had been invited to join the family in private, she chose the main chapel and the other mourners wondered why. If pride prevented her from doing so, it did nothing to conceal the red and swollen eyes beneath a thin black veil.

Those who observed her that day said no one else showed the grief she openly displayed, disrupting the service before it began. In her own deliberate way, she dominated the chapel by not sitting in the back pews or with the family out of sight. Miss Barbara Stanwyck was there to mourn the man she loved. 'There will be no other man in my life,' she said when they divorced.

Robert Taylor was dead.

The eulogy was given by his closest friend, Governor Ronald Reagan, who barely made it through without breaking down as he spoke the words: 'Bob loved his home and everything that it meant. Above all he loved his family, and his beautiful (wife) Ursula, little Tessa and his son Terry in whom he had so much pride.'

Barbara's sobbing affected Reagan's ability to continue. Finally he turned to the family vestibule: 'Bob spoke to me a few days ago. I am sure he meant for me to tell you something that he wanted above all else. Ursula, there is just one thing that only you can do for him – be happy. This was his last thought to me.'

Every heart in the chapel stirred for the hidden Ursula, but it was Stanwyck who drew all the attention. When Reagan completed his eulogy, no one moved until Barbara stood up and almost in a faint was ushered out of the church. As flashbulbs flashed in her face, she nearly passed out.

Tom Purvis, Taylor's Navy buddy, was relieved when she

finally got into a limousine. He had known Bob for twenty-five years, but had seen Barbara only once or twice. 'She didn't like me and I didn't like her for no particular reason other than she resented all his friends. They weren't welcome in the house when she was married to Bob. Why the hell she came to the funeral in such a pitiful state, I don't know.

'We were all invited to the Taylor house for a "drink on him," a Hollywood tradition after the funeral. I was shocked when Barbara walked in. Bob would not have wanted this, but Ursula had made the polite gesture. She probably didn't think Barbara would accept but she did and she was heavily sedated or drunk. When she left I felt we could relax and talk about the good times, but then I looked out the front window and saw Barbara with Ursula. There we were, a group of men peering out from behind the curtains to make sure Ursula was all right. She and Barbara walked round and round the circular driveway and Barbara was doing all the talking. About what, everyone wanted to know but never found out.'

The private conversation ended under a magnolia tree, all eyes waiting for a display of tears. But the two women just parted, no brief hug or handshake. To the relief of everyone, Barbara's limousine eased down the dusty driveway and disappeared.

Ursula was not upset and indicated that Stanwyck was not at all the way Bob described her. Why did he go out of his way to avoid her? 'You don't know Barbara the way I do,' he said and left it at that. Ursula learned the hard way that Bob was right when she found out that Barbara billed his estate for alimony to the day he died. Everyone assumed she understood that medical and hospital bills drained Taylor's cash reserve. She visited him only once when he was dying and promised to waive her fifteen per cent of his salary for the nine months he was suffering from lung cancer.

Barbara was a very wealthy woman, but she needed this one last link to Taylor, possessing him like a widow to the very end.

Stanwyck was tough. She was one of the few movie legends who was not moulded by a Hollywood studio as was the custom in the Golden Era. Her independence as an actress matched her independence as a woman. She was categorised with Bette Davis, who might have been more popular at the box office, but admittedly gave some bad performances. Barbara, however, remained on an even keel as an actress. No matter how dreadful the script, she never failed to come through admirably. Bette used her influence in Hollywood with a dynamic flare of temperament. Barbara used her power with an unyielding composure of a lioness. Her five-foot-five frame stood taller than her leading men and her diminutive one hundred and fifteen pounds outweighed the most oppressive movie director.

Early on Stanwyck accepted the mirror's reflection of a plain girl with ordinary features and skinny figure. Her life revolved around her acting ability rather than glamour and she cared less about her hair and wardrobe. For one of her films she put a dress on backwards and was on camera before anyone noticed. She concentrated on her work and started a new film by not only memorising her own dialogue, but everyone else's lines, entrances and exits, as well. For some actors her prompting was annoying while others were grateful. Actor Laurence Harvey said, 'I never knew which side of the camera Stanwyck was working. Actress or director.' She usually stayed on the movie set whether she was needed or not. While most actresses eased their boredom between takes by doing needlepoint, knitting or reading, Barbara observed the action to keep in rhythm with the storyline. She had no hobbies and rarely took a vacation. Pride did not prevent her from accepting parts that had been turned down by other actresses. If she liked the script, nothing else mattered. She never took an acting lesson. She possessed an inborn talent that required a minimum of coaching.

Her screen persona reflected the hardships she endured during her childhood and early adult life. She never completely shed her Brooklyn accent, but modified it into a dialect that typified Barbara Stanwyck. Her forte was the downtrodden woman fighting for respectability, but she was also convincing as a stripper, a deceitful conniving wife, a card shark, a gun moll, and western heroine.

Stanwyck could play many roles effectively on and off the screen. Actor Clifton Webb referred to her as 'my favourite lesbian'. Was she or wasn't she? Boze Hadleigh, author of *Hollywood Lesbians* asked Barbara face to face. He showed her his list and her name was on top. She promptly threw him out of her house. A few of her girlfriends, actresses Marjorie Main, Joan Crawford and Agnes Moorhead, were also mentioned. In *The Girls: Sappho Goes to Hollywood* author Diana McLellan writes that Oscar-winning actress Tallulah Bankhead told MGM mogul Louis B. Mayer that she had slept with several of his biggest stars, these included Stanwyck and Crawford who confirmed this to Mayer at a cocktail party. I asked Joan about this, feigning outrage. She smiled and replied, 'Same sex relations is common in Hollywood. One has to do it to get ahead.' Writer and producer Joe Mankiewicz commented, 'Everyone in Hollywood is bisexual.'

Popular actor Cesar Romero told Boze Hadleigh there were so many beautiful people in Hollywood gender didn't matter. The charming and distinguished Cesar, who was Tyrone Power's lover, frequently escorted Barbara to important events.

Most likely Stanwyck was bisexual and not a lesbian because of her great love and devotion to her husbands Frank Fay and, in particular, Robert Taylor. She had affairs with director Frank Capra, and actor Robert Wagner, and flings with other men including Humphry Bogart, Gary Cooper and William Holden. Lesbians and homosexuals did get married and had children to protect their images, but this was not the case with Barbara.

In 2006 we read excerpts from William J. Mann's biography of Katharine Hepburn in *Vanity Fair* that revealed she and Spencer Tracy were bisexual, and rarely if ever were intimate with each other but their chemistry on the screen was worth millions and so were their reputations. Hepburn, like Greta Garbo and Marlene Dietrich, wore men's clothes before it was acceptable because they cared less what people thought but Stanwyck wanted very much to be accepted. Her rough exterior made her popular with lesbians who admired her lack of pretence and frills, her military walk of confidence and her husky voice. In films she was at her best using and abusing men despite the fact she wasn't beautiful or buxom. She seduced them with blasé mannerisms and suggestive dialogue that was tinged with hatred for the opposite sex. As Lily in *Baby Face* she sleeps her way up to the penthouse, destroying every man who stands in her way. Wearing a blonde wig as Phyllis Dietrichson in *Double Indemnity* she convinces Fred MacMurray to kill her husband for the insurance money and as Martha Wilkison in *The Violent Men* she abandons husband Edward G. Robinson bound in a wheelchair to die in a house fire.

Stanwyck grew up fast. She had no choice. 'I'm a tough old broad from Brooklyn,' she said. How far is it from the dirty streets in New York to the elegant Trousdale Estates in Los Angeles, California?

CHAPTER ONE

Ruby

Barbara Stanwyck was born Ruby Stevens on 16 July 1907, in Brooklyn, New York. Her mother Catherine McGee, who had black hair and violet eyes, grew up in Chelsea, Massachusetts, where her Irish immigrant parents settled. She married a handsome, red-headed fisherman, Byron Stevens, when she was twenty years old. Daughters Maude and Mabel were born less than a year apart, followed by Mildred, then Malcolm Byron in 1905. Catherine stayed home to take care of the children while her husband tried to make a living from the sea. When the fish weren't biting, he found odd jobs in construction and became an expert bricklayer. Byron was a restless man and a heavy drinker who was known for his Jekyll and Hyde personality. He could be quiet and understanding, but more often his temper flared. He resented being poor and tied down, having to struggle to support a wife and four children. He listened to the sailors who came into the port of Chelsea describing life in the big cities where job opportunities were better and, without any warning, deserted his family one night in 1905.

Catherine had many reasons for wanting him back. She was a devout Catholic and believed in the sanctity of marriage, and he was the man she loved and the father of her children, who needed food, clothes and shelter. By talking to the men who worked with her husband, she found out he was working as a bricklayer in Brooklyn.

There was nothing Byron could do when Catherine and the children showed up. He was enjoying life as a single man and resented having to settle down again, but Catherine set up housekeeping at 246 Classon Avenue in Brooklyn. Maude and Mabel got married and moved out, easing the financial burden on Byron, but then Catherine discovered she was pregnant again. It was early 1907, Byron was out of work, and the pressure began to build up once more. On 16 July, Ruby Catherine was born.

The Stevens children lived in an environment of poverty. They thought the train whistles down the street were something all children heard in the middle of the night. Although they were punished if they dared to cross the railroad tracks, they were allowed to walk down to the waterfront and watch the ships sailing in and out of port. It was cool there and if they pretended hard enough, for a while they could forget the garbage and clothes lines at home. In this neighbourhood, women in their twenties looked thirty years older as they scrubbed floors with torn rags, cooked in huge black pots, and carried their newborn babies under one arm while they hung up cloth nappies that never got clean.

Two years after Ruby was born, Catherine found out she was pregnant with her sixth child. Soon to give birth in 1910, she was stepping off a trolley car when she was accidentally pushed in the street, hitting her head on the pavement. She died a month later. Byron leaned heavily on the bottle to get through the funeral but was unable to cope with the prospect of his future as a single parent, solely responsible for the family. He signed up to work on the Panama Canal and his children never saw him again.

Mildred, who had been working as a chorus girl, knew her father would not send money to support Ruby and Byron. She looked to Mabel and Maude for help, but they had problems of their own so the youngest siblings were placed in foster homes a few blocks apart. At five, young Byron was concerned about his little sister who disappeared every afternoon; he soon found out that three-year-old Ruby was playing in front of 246 Classon Avenue, looking for her mother.

'It wasn't quite as bad as it sounded,' Stanwyck recalled. 'In those days foster homes were not cruel; they were just impersonal.'

Mildred travelled as a dancer but continued to support her brother and sister, enjoying her visits with them whenever she was in New York. When Ruby was about five, Mildred told her and Byron that their father had died at sea. The youngsters did not give up hope but later, Stanwyck faced a bigger challenge: 'I could almost accept being shuffled from one strange home to another and even the death of my father whom I never knew, but when I was eight, my whole world fell apart. Mildred thought Byron was old enough to live with her. I pleaded, but she took him anyway.'

Ruby had to face the world alone now, and that's precisely what she did. Without Byron to protect her, she fought her own battles on the street, used foul language and became a rebellious child. She had no friends and did not bond with her foster parents. 'I usually slept on a living-room cot, went to school, and played in the streets. I was a stupid brat,' Barbara recalled.

The other little girls did not like Ruby and she, in turn, did not like them. She was a scrapper and a whiz at playing street games with the boys, who liked her spunk and snappy answers.

During the summer Mildred went on the road with Ruby who picked up whatever dance steps she could, practising faithfully every day. Having made up her mind to be a dancer, she considered school a waste of time.

When she was twelve, Ruby went to live with the Cohen family who looked upon her as more than a foster child. 'Not only was the house clean, but it was full of sincere love and they were always concerned about me,' Stanwyck said. 'I wasn't sent to school without my hair being combed, my face scrubbed and without clean clothes. The Cohens were rather poor, but they fed me well, took me to church and sometimes to the movies.'

Maybe the Cohens were able to make Ruby look like a little lady, but they couldn't teach her to talk like one. Every other sentence contained a curse word, and though reprimanded every time she swore, using obscene language became part of her personality. However, despite herself, Ruby changed for the better during her two years with the only family she had ever known.

When Mrs Cohen became pregnant, Ruby did not have to be told there would be no room for her now. At 14, she quit school, lied about her age and made money by wrapping packages, office filing and cutting out dress patterns at Abraham and Strauss in Brooklyn. 'I hated those jobs,' Stanwyck recalled. She wanted to be a dancer but Mildred wouldn't allow it so she applied for a job as a typist at the Remick Music Publishing Company on 48th Street in Manhattan. Ruby spent her spare time with Mildred and her boyfriend, James 'Buck' Mack, referred to fondly by Ruby as Uncle Buck, who persuaded Mildred to allow her little sister to audition as a dancer at the Strand Theater in Times Square. She got the job, which paid 35 dollars a week, and her first professional training as a dancer from director Earl Lindsay.

At 16, Ruby became the most reliable girl in the chorus line. She was able to handle men who got fresh with her by cursing in their language. She had auburn hair and blue eyes, was too thin with few curves but she had the energy and the will to succeed, and believed if she moved fast and kicked high enough, her figure wasn't important. Ruby was like her father – rough, restless, loud, sarcastic and always on the defensive, but as she gained confidence, she loosened up and became friendly with dancers, Mae Clarke and Wanda Mansfield. They shared a coldwater flat on 46th Street between Fifth and Sixth Avenues.

'We lived over a laundry that could be steamy at times and especially hot during the summer,' Stanwyck said. 'The heat seemed to come through every crack in the floor and ceiling. Then there was the noisy Sixth Avenue El that shook the walls. We were in a glamorous business, so we couldn't allow our dates to see the joint. We told them to drop us off at one of the hotels in the theatre district and pretended we lived there.'

When the show at the Strand closed, the girls went to work for Earl Lindsay at the Morosco Theater in *Keep Kool* that opened on 22 May 1924. Ruby was one of the 'Keep Kool Cuties' who inspired a critic at *Variety* to write: 'These sixteen girls are pips, lookers and dancers. They kick like steers and look like why-men-leave-home in their many costume flashes.'

When the show closed in late August, some of the sketches were used in the touring company of *Ziegfeld Follies*. Ruby was offered a hundred dollars a week to go on the road in the 'Ziegfeld Shadowgraph' number doing a striptease behind a white screen. 'I tossed my clothes out into the audience,' Stanwyck said. 'But if they didn't wear three-dimensional glasses, they didn't get to see anything.' She was stark naked.

The Roaring Twenties were in high gear and Ruby Stevens was in the hub of speakeasies, bootleg booze, gangsters, stage-door johnnies, short skirts and low necklines, fast music, fast girls, sugar daddies and botched abortions. Stanwyck did not document these years beyond her dancing so we'll never know how she behaved off stage.

Following the Ziegfeld tour, Ruby worked at Anatole Friedland's Club on 54th Street. Six months later, she and Mae Clarke accepted Earl Lindsay's offer to appear in a Shubert revue, *Gay Paree*, with Ruth Gillette and Billy Van. To earn extra money, the girls danced at a little after-hours dump called the Everglades Club. They ran from one job to the other in the bitter cold of January 1926, sometimes wearing only a coat over their underwear and flimsy shoes without stockings. Ruby danced the Black Bottom in the 1926 version of George White's *Scandals* at the Apollo. She was also on call as a dance instructor at a speakeasy for gays and lesbians, owned by Texas Guinan's brother, that was raided by the vice squad when Ruby was giving a tango lesson. She said in later years that she wasn't a great dancer but knew her left foot from the right.

Ruby hung out at The Tavern on 48th Street, mingling with other show-business people. The owner, Billy LaHiff, was sympathetic to young hopefuls and allowed them to run up a tab or fed them for free. Aware that producer-director Willard Mack needed chorus girls for his new play, *The Noose*, Billy introduced him to Ruby, and Mack offered her a job. One version of this story has her sticking her neck out by asking him if he needed any more dancers.

'Yeah, three or four,' he replied.

Ruby motioned to her roommates and said, 'We all need jobs. All of us or nobody.'

In later years, Stanwyck did not mention Mae and Wanda

when retelling this story, only that Mack had told her the part had been cast in New York but she could have it out of town. However, Mae got a small part in the second act, but Wanda didn't make it.

Willard Mack was born Charles Willard McLaughlin in Ontario, Canada, on 18 September 1873. He was one of the most prolific dramatists of his time. He wrote 23 Broadway plays, performed in 10 of them and was producer of 4. His first wife was the well-known stage beauty, Maude Leone. She divorced him in 1910 and two years later he married actress Marjorie Rambeau. They divorced in 1916 and the following year he married the beautiful stage actress, Pauline Frederick, who seduced Clark Gable when he had a bit part in one of her plays. After she divorced Mack in 1919, he married Beatrice Banyard, who was tutored by him and became a successful actress and writer. This marriage lasted until his death in 1934.

Mack wrote plays for his famous wives and brought out the best of their talents. Though three divorced him, he said they were justified: 'I drank too much and I'm difficult to get along with.'

The Pittsburgh tryout debut of *The Noose* was a disaster, so Mack revised the script and shuffled the cast into different roles. Ruby had a few lines in the original play but Mack decided to give her a bigger part. His attraction to Ruby sorted her out from the other chorus girls who were equally capable of reciting a few lines. She was not well spoken, had no acting experience and walked like a Russian soldier, but Mack liked her. She was ambitious, had spirit and was eager to learn and, although he was smitten with her, he was no fool. The success of *The Noose* was more important than their love affair. With his guidance, Ruby might be able to save his play.

'Willard Mack showed me all the tricks, how to sell myself

with entrances and exits,' Stanwyck said. 'Only through his kindness and patience did I make it through. He completely rearranged my mental make-up. It was a rebirth for me and damn painful for him to put up with me. I was temperamental because I was scared. I told him I couldn't act. It was hopeless. I couldn't act and what's more, I wouldn't act. Then he did a turn-about and, in front of the entire company, he said I was a chorus girl and would always be a chorus girl, would live like a chorus girl and . . . "To hell with you!" I thought. It worked. I yelled back at him that I could act, would act and was not just a chorus girl!'

Before signing her to a contract, Mack told her, 'Ruby Stevens sounds like the name of a chorus girl, not an actress.' He looked through an old English theatre programme that listed Jane Stanwyck in *Barbara Frietchie*. Almost immediately, he came out with it. 'From now on, you'll be known as Barbara Stanwyck.' As she was about to sign her name she got as far as 'Bar', looked up at Mack and asked, 'How do you spell Barbara?' From then on she always signed her first name with two capital Bs, as in BarBara.

CHAPTER TWO

BarBara

If Mack had doubts about Barbara, he never admitted it, even to himself, but her facing a New York audience for the first time was a nerve-wracking event for him. He rehearsed her relentlessly, night and day. 'Except for catnaps backstage, I didn't sleep at all,' she said. 'He hammered every line, every inflection and every gesture of the part into my memory. I was too tired and too terrified to think for myself. All I could do was go, like a robot, through the part as he told me to. Toward the end I broke down and wept with exhaustion. I told him it was no use.' Mack exclaimed, 'You'll do it when the time comes because you'll have to.'

The Noose opened on 20 October 1926 at the Hudson Theater on Broadway. It was a smash hit. The *New York Telegram* said: 'There is an uncommonly fine performance by Barbara Stanwyck, who not only does the Charleston steps of a dance-hall girl gracefully, but knows how to act, a feature which somehow with her comely looks seems kind of superfluous. After this girl breaks down and sobs out her unrequited love for the young bootlegger in that genuinely moving scene in the last act, of course, there is nothing for the governor to do but reprieve the boy. If he hadn't, the weeping audience would probably have yelled at him until he did.'

Billboard raved: 'Barbara Stanwyck is splendid as the leader of the little chorus and she achieves real heights in her brief emotional scene.'

The *New York Sun* reported that Stanwyck made first-nighters wipe tears from their eyes. *The New York Times* referred to her as Dorothy Stanwyck, but said she did 'good work'.

Stanwyck was more relieved than excited and Mack did not offer too much praise until she answered one very important question. Did she want to become a good actress or continue dancing? Her answer didn't surprise him.

'I want to be an actress,' she replied.

Without a smile Mack said, 'Then we have a lot of work to do.'

Though *The Noose* ran on Broadway for nine months, they rehearsed her lines each morning, and he gave her a different play to study with him every week.

At 19, Barbara was attractive. There was a softness about her that was wistful and innocent despite the fast life she had led as a showgirl. She stopped running with flashy admirers after she began dating a young man by the name of Edward Kennedy (no relation to the JFK family), but she changed her mind about marrying him when she became an actress. He suspected she was having an affair with Willard Mack. Her good friend Joan Crawford said she did, but Barbara would never admit to it. She said she was in love with her leading man in *The Noose*, Rex Cherryman, who played the part of the doomed bootlegger. At 28, he was one of Broadway's finest young actors.

Born in Grand Rapids, Michigan on 30 October 1896,

Cherryman made a film, *Madam Peacock*, with Alla Nazimova in 1920 before turning to the stage. In 1924 he made his New York debut with Willard Mack's former wife, Marjorie Rambeau, in *The Valley of Content*.

Rex was married to Esther Lamb, who was in the process of divorcing him, and they had a son. He was extraordinarily handsome and had a wonderful sense of humour. Women chased him and he took advantage of it until he became intrigued with Barbara. Her shy, unpretentious manner was refreshing to Cherryman who had been dating beautiful and sophisticated actresses. He and Stanwyck became a steady couple and as she described it later, 'It was all so perfect. We were both becoming established Broadway performers and understood each other very well.'

While still appearing in *The Noose*, Stanwyck was approached by Hollywood film producer, Robert Kane, to make a screen test at the old Cosmospolitan Studios on 125th Street and Second Avenue for the silent film *Broadway Nights*, the story of a woman in a roller-coaster marriage. Stanwyck said it was a horrible experience because the cameraman tried to seduce her while she was attempting to get into the mood for the test. The director Charles Boyle ignored the situation and explained to her that the part she was trying out for, called for her to cry. 'When I say "action", let's see some tears,' he said casually.

Even though Barbara cried every night on stage in *The Noose*, she couldn't do it on camera. Boyle gave her a raw onion, but nothing happened. She failed the test, but got a small part as a fan dancer.

The Noose closed in June 1927. A few weeks later, Stanwyck auditioned for George Manker Watter's Broadway play, *Burlesque*. 'She is what I wanted,' producer-director Arthur

Hopkins said. 'Stanwyck had a rough poignancy and displayed sensitivity and emotion far superior to some of the great actresses I've known.' Barbara's role as Bonny, the wife of a drunken vaudevillian, played by Hal Skelly, who leaves him but returns to help him regain his pride, was a demanding one. *Burlesque* opened on 1 September 1927 at the Plymouth Theater and was a hit.

Willard Mack had taught Barbara the fundamentals of the stage, and director Arthur Hopkins showed her how to 'feel' the part. 'He never really told me what to do,' she said. 'He told me stories and let me imagine how it should be and how I should feel in these particular situations. Then I went about it by following my own instincts.'

Alexander Woollcott reviewed *Burlesque* in *The World*: 'Miss Stanwyck's performance was touching and true and she brought much to those little aching silences in a performance of which Mr Hopkins knows so well, the secret of the sorcery.' Brooks Atkinson in *The New York Times* said: 'Hal Skelly's high-spirited performance of the slapdash comic and Barbara Stanwyck's quietly sincere interpretation of the music-hall wife are joys to behold.'

Barbara, coached by Hopkins, told *New York Review* that pity is akin to love, 'and I suppose that has a great deal to do with Bonny's feeling toward her husband in the play . . . I have often thought of what the finish would be for these two people – what old age would bring to them.'

Stanwyck eventually suffered Bonny's fate in real life, sacrificing her pride for a drunken clown until love and pity turned to hatred.

At the age of 21, Barbara was more polished on stage than off. It took time to transform Ruby Stevens into Barbara Stanwyck.

Later in life, when she was one of the most sought after actresses in the world, she confessed that expressing herself was difficult and often impossible. Tact was not one of her virtues. Though life was treating her well in 1928, she remembered a lesson she had learned as a foster child living with the Cohen family – it was too good to last.

Her career was flourishing and Rex Cherryman proposed marriage. She could not ask for more from life. But then Rex became ill when he was performing in *The Trial of Mary Dugan* with Ann Harding. Doctors recommended a complete rest and suggested an ocean voyage. In those days physicians thought the sea air could cure anything. Barbara went with Rex to the French Line pier and promised to join him in Paris soon. On 10 August 1928, Cherryman died of septic poisoning shortly before the steamer *De Grasse* arrived at Le Havre. His wishes to be cremated were carried out and his ashes interred in France.

Barbara was devastated, but she had little time to grieve. Actors say the show must go on and she believed this. Work was her salvation. The *Burlesque* cast rallied around Stanwyck and tried to keep her occupied when she was not performing.

Piano player Oscar Levant arranged for her to watch comedian Frank Fay from the wings of the Palace Theater and introduced them after the show. Barbara was disgusted by Fay's inflated ego. She told Levant, 'It's real apparent he loves himself. He's his own biggest fan and never shuts up.' Oscar reminded her that Fay was the hottest thing on Broadway and breaking all records at the Palace.

'Yeah?' she smirked. 'That doesn't mean I have to like him.'

Levant passed along her comment to Frank who sarcastically retorted, 'She's nothing to get excited about either.'

However, Fay reminded Barbara of her father Byron who had red hair, a fierce Irish temper, a hyper personality and a restless soul. Though she was only three when she walked with Byron behind her mother's coffin the memory of him on that dark day remained with her.

When Cherryman was alive, he and Barbara often ran into Fay on the nightclub circuit, and they kept up a sarcastic flow of bantering barbs and counter barbs. They knew the language of the street and it was no-holds-barred, each vying for the last insult. 'I can't stand him,' she told anyone within hearing range.

Divorced twice, Frank loved women and enjoyed bragging about his conquests, but he had rarely met anyone, especially a woman, who could keep up with him. He swore like a trooper, but she turned the air blue. Always on stage, he told one joke after another and she never missed a punchline. Fay had met his match and began to look forward to seeing Barbara and exchanging wits with her. He was fascinated by her earthy personality and bluntness.

But it was not until Cherryman's death that Frank Fay came to Stanwyck as a friend and someone who was sincerely interested in helping her through the dark days. When she needed him, he was there. He listened patiently and sympathetically to her talking endlessly about Rex until she got it out of her system. She found herself leaning on Fay, who had known for some time that he was falling in love with her. She was too broken-hearted to realise her feelings for him, but she was in awe of Frank once she got to know him better because he knew who he was and where he was going. His confidence gave her the courage to move on. Just as rewarding was discovering that there was another side to this cocky show-off.

CHAPTER THREE

Broadway's Favourite Son

Francis Anthony Fay, suave archetype of the old Palace guard, was born to a vaudeville couple in San Francisco on 17 November 1896. He was in show business from the age of four – a master of the studied insult, the raised eyebrow that could turn into a ribald double entendre, the droll aside that stung like a whiplash. His parody of the song 'Tea for Two' (Who wants to bake a cake at three in the morning?) was a classic.

Fay made his stage debut as a potato bug, elf or teddy bear – nobody could remember which – in Victor Herbert's *Babes in Toyland*. He did road shows in the Midwest and made his Broadway debut in *The Passing Show of 1918* with Fred and Adele Astaire. He was married briefly to Ziegfeld Follies beauty, Frances White. His second wife Gladys Lee Buchanan also divorced him. In 1921 Fay hit rock bottom and filed a voluntary petition in bankruptcy. He claimed his only assets were his clothes worth $100.

By developing the role of master of ceremonies into an art of wit, Fay made a comeback and in 1926 played the Palace for a hundred continuous performances, breaking all records. His stooge was Patsy Kelly, who eventually made good in Hollywood as a comedienne.

He wasn't much liked by other comics. Milton Berle said, 'You can count Fay's friends on the missing arm of a one-armed man. He was too full of himself and arrogant.'

In court on a business matter, the opposing attorney asked for his profession. Frank replied, 'I am the greatest comedian in the world.'

Later his attorney criticised him for the answer.

Fay looked stunned. 'I was under oath, wasn't I?'

Frank was a complex, fascinating, compelling fellow off stage. Though he attended Mass every day, he was more of a superstitious Catholic than a religious one. He wore a St Christopher's medal around his neck, and always tipped his hat when he passed a house of worship. He also read his horoscope every day and when asked if he had more faith in God or astrology, Fay replied, 'I'm just covering all the bases.' There was no happy medium for Frank Fay. He was either rich or broke, dead drunk or dead sober. Anything in-between was dull to him.

He collected everything from antiques to unwashed socks worn by baseball heroes. On stage he dressed in expensive flamboyant robes, but in private he enjoyed leaning back in an easy chair wearing only a pair of shorts.

Frank Fay was the sort of guy Ruby Stevens might have met on the street in Brooklyn: Irish Catholic, rough and tumble, big-mouthed and cocksure. He became her idol; she adored him. But Frank made it very clear that he was the star, not her. When Metro-Goldwyn Studio boss Louis B. Mayer expressed an interest in Barbara, after seeing *Burlesque*, she wasn't interested. This wasn't the only movie offer she turned down and Oscar Levant wanted to know why. 'Because Frank wouldn't like it,' Barbara told him.

Less than ten weeks after Rex Cherryman's death, Stanwyck boarded a train for St Louis where Fay was working as emcee at the Missouri Theater. Fay had proposed to Barbara on the telephone. She was missing him terribly and terrified of losing the security she had found with him. He was offering her the salvation and love that she had been seeking all her life. They were married on 26 August 1928 and Stanwyck would give of herself completely to the man who, she was sure, would be her husband forever.

The newlyweds had one strike against them, though – Frank's monumental ego. He did not want any competition in the marriage. If Barbara was going to remain in show business it would be on his terms, and she was not to accept any offers without his approval.

Problems began almost immediately for the Fays when there was talk that Stanwyck would play the lead in the silent film version of *Burlesque* for Paramount Pictures in Hollywood. Fay told her not to consider it until he had time to follow through with some offers of his own. If they went to Hollywood, it would be because the great Frank Fay was in demand.

Barbara was approached by Joseph Schenck, head of United Artists, about doing *The Locked Door*, a film adaptation of Channing Pollock's popular play, *The Sign on the Locked Door*. She refused to discuss it until Frank signed a contract with Warner Brothers to host the star-studded musical, *Show of Shows*. 'I'm going to take Hollywood by storm,' Fay bragged. 'If they need people with stage presence, I'm their guy. Broadway's favourite son!'

Hollywood was still going through a difficult transition from silent films to talkies. The careers of many actors whose voices were not acceptable were ruined, so the major studios looked to actors on the stage to replace their fallen stars.

In March 1929, the Fays travelled to California with Joe Schenck in his private railroad car. Frank didn't stop talking about himself and how he was going to contribute the talent of a lifetime to movies and save them single-handedly from oblivion. Barbara remained in the background, always giving her husband centre stage.

It's a shame Frank didn't shut his mouth during the four-day trip. Schenck wasn't the least bit impressed by him. But Barbara was impressed with the welcoming committee waiting for the movie mogul at Union Station. Mary Pickford, Douglas Fairbanks, MGM's boy genius Irving Thalberg, and the press, were there to shake hands with the returning Schenck, who had been in New York for only three weeks. Frank naively thought they were paying homage to him. Barbara knew better, of course, and was touched by the friendliness of it, but agreed with her husband that the palm trees and warmth of California weren't for them. It did not take long for them to miss the hustle and bustle of New York City and the neon lights of Broadway.

The next morning Barbara reported to United Artists to meet George Fitzmaurice, director of *The Locked Door*. He was well known for his work with stunning actresses Pola Negri, Norma Talmadge, Billie Dove and Vilma Banky. As he was fussing with draperies behind Barbara, Fitzmaurice focused on her and commented, 'Damn. I can't make you beautiful no matter what I do. Nothing helps.'

Barbara might have been hurt, but instead she put him in his place. 'You sent for me. I didn't send for you.'

Though Fitzmaurice was a good director he had his doubts about sound and proving himself all over again. This was the general feeling in Hollywood at that time. Placing microphones in potted plants and centrepieces was a distraction that forced the director to focus on the quality of voices and background noises instead of important camera angles, dialogue and plot. The successful movies in the early era of sound, *The Jazz Singer* and *Broadway Melody of 1929*, were both musicals that did not require the attention to the actors in a drama. Fitzmaurice was more concerned about his reputation as a director and technical problems than he was about teaching a newcomer the art of making films. Stanwyck had been trained to project her voice and exaggerate her body movements for the stage. No one bothered to show her how to tone these down for the microphone and camera.

In *The Locked Door*, Barbara portrayed the kind of woman she would play often – the gal with a dark past. Married to her boss (William 'Stage' Boyd), she is faced with exposure when a former boyfriend (Rod La Rocque) shows up. The husband shoots her ex-lover, and she is blamed, but the bad guy lives to tell the truth.

The Locked Door was terrible, but the *New York Herald Tribune* reported that 'Barbara Stanwyck gives an honest and moving picture as the distraught wife . . . it is in every way an excellent piece of work.' *The New York Times* thought Barbara 'acquits herself favorably'.

'They never should have unlocked that damned thing,' Barbara said years later.

Disappointed with her Hollywood debut, Stanwyck made several screen tests, but heard nothing. 'Nobody bothered to train me,' she said. 'In the theatre I had to reach the guys in the balcony and my arms and legs were stretched to accommodate the size of the stage. But on a small movie set, my voice was shrill and I was awkward. I was lost. Who the hell was going to teach me in this dizzy town?'

Her next film, *Mexicali Rose*, was worse. She played a Mexican girl, who is murdered for being unfaithful.

For a twenty-three-year-old girl who started out with nothing, yet managed to become a fine stage actress, Barbara felt she had made a terrible mistake trying to break into films and was afraid that her first two failed attempts might ruin her chances of acting again, either in movies or on the stage. A feeling of helplessness smothered her ambition and confidence.

Frank Fay used his influence at Warner Brothers to get her a screen test, but the studio did not provide her with a script, make-up man or director. She knew they were merely going through the motions. Finally a man appeared on the set and asked her what she wanted to do for the test. Totally unprepared, Barbara did a scene from *The Noose*. When she finished, the man had tears in his eyes. He came over to her and said, 'It doesn't mean anything coming from me, I'm leaving Hollywood a failure. But I want you to know it's been a privilege I won't forget.'

'Then he kissed my hand,' Barbara recalled. 'I will always be grateful to that man. Incidentally, that "failure" was to win a knighthood for his great screen achievements.'

But the front office at Warner Brothers did not think Alexander Korda or Barbara Stanwyck had anything to offer the movie industry. For six months she was just the wife of Frank Fay, a big star busy making *Show of Shows*. The film was a huge success and Fay, of course, took most of the credit, even though he was only one of 77 stars of stage and screen participating. As master of ceremonies he was bright-eyed, masterful, quick and funny. *The New York Times* wrote, 'Fay is excellent.'

His next two films, *Under a Texas Moon* and *The Matrimonial Bed* were also good. He was riding high and pleased to have Barbara waiting for him at home after a busy day at the studio. If she was depressed by the situation, it would pass, he decided. He intended to be successful enough for both of them.

Barbara convinced herself she was satisfied being Mrs Frank Fay. Every night they went to a swanky party or were invited out for dinner. It was all part of the game. Besides, Stanwyck didn't know how to cook . . .

As the months passed, however, Fay was forced to face facts. His wife was very now depressed and her moods were affecting their marriage. She had no energy or desire for anything, and Frank's enthusiasm made her more sullen. Very much in love with Barbara, he wanted her to come to life again. So what if she worked once in a while, he thought. He approached the head of Columbia Studios, the sarcastic and ruthless Harry Cohn, and offered to pay Barbara's salary and expenses if they would give her a chance. Cohn said he might be able to use her in *Ladies of Leisure*, but she would have to go through the routine interview with director Frank Capra.

Frank rushed home to tell Barbara who screamed at him, 'Forget it! I'm not interested.'

'You gotta go over there now,' he exclaimed. 'They're waitin' for ya!'

'Yeah? Well, I can't take any more of this town. They don't want me and I don't want them!'

'C'mon, honey. Don't embarrass me. Get dressed and get going!'

Barbara dragged herself off the couch and shuffled to the door.

'You can't go lookin' like that!' Fay said. 'Change your dress, comb your hair and put on some lipstick.'

'What's the use?' she sighed going through the motions.

When Stanwyck walked into Frank Capra's office, she was the living embodiment of her two bad performances in *The Locked Door* and *Mexicali Rose* – drab and sullen. She slumped into a chair with a weary and bored expression on her face.

Capra asked several questions about her background and she mumbled a few words. He was disgusted with her, but followed through with the usual, 'You'll have to make a screen test.'

Suddenly Barbara's temper flared and she jumped out of the chair. 'Oh, hell, you don't want any part of me!' she hissed and stormed out of the office. Capra was furious, grabbed the phone and called Harry Cohn. 'About that Stanwyck girl,' he growled. 'She's not an actress. She's a porcupine!'

Barbara arrived home in tears – six months of frustration coming to the surface. Frank wanted to know about the interview with Capra, but she continued to sob, unable to catch her breath. Fay suspected the worst. Obviously Capra made a pass at her. In a rage he called Harry Cohn. 'What the hell did Capra do to my wife?'

'That dame's got a chip on her shoulder,' Cohn shot back. 'Capra's a gentleman, for Christ's sake! He tried to talk to her, that's all. Not only did she look like hell, she acted like a spoiled brat. Capra called her a porcupine, and do you know why, Fay? She turned her back on him . . . ran out of the office and slammed the door in his face! Forget the whole thing.'

Frank calmed down because Cohn's description of Barbara's tantrum was typical of her these days. 'She was a success on Broadway,' he explained. 'I dragged her out here and she's been knocked around and insulted. She doesn't have faith in anyone and I'm beginning to think she doesn't have faith in me. I got one favour to ask and you can't turn me down. I'm gonna show you a test Barbara did at Warner's.'

Cohn was the kind of guy to hang up or say, 'Go to hell!' in situations like this, but he was also shrewd. If he wanted to use Fay in a movie some time, the comic would be obligated to him.

Later, Capra said that Stanwyck had so many strikes against her he had made up his mind to hate the three-minute test when he sat down in the projection room, but seldom had he been so impressed and he asked Cohn to sign Barbara for *Ladies of Leisure* as the party girl engaged to a society artist (Ralph Graves). She chases him for his money but falls in love and tries to hide her wicked past. The cheap wisecracks and heavy make-up in the beginning and then the gradual transition to a gracious lady who wants to be worthy of the man she loves is vintage Stanwyck. 'Well, brother, that's my racket. I'm a party girl.'

Ladies of Leisure began filming on 14 January 1930. Capra discovered almost immediately that the girl who ran out of his office was not the girl who reported for work that day. The other Barbara – the real Barbara – was full of energy and spirit, anxious and willing, determined and alert. After shooting a few scenes he studied her on film. The make-up men were attempting to make her more attractive and that was not what he wanted. The following day he told her not to worry about looking beautiful because that wasn't possible. 'No make-up,' he instructed. 'Just be yourself.'

Capra also noted she was at her best on the first take. In the second and third, she was stiff and forced. The other cast members resented his decision to rehearse without Barbara and having to do a scene more than once because on the first take the camera focused on her. It meant more work for them but Capra, to his delight, had found a virgin film actress and a unique one at that. She knew very little about making movies and listened carefully to everything he told her, but when they watched the rushes at the end of the day, Barbara complained that she was awkward and ugly. 'If you succeed in Hollywood it will be for your acting ability and not your face,' he said bluntly. 'By being so self-conscious you've lost your spontaneity and naturalness.' He made her promise she would never look at the daily rushes again, and she never did.

Capra had become her God, her Svengali, her strength – and her lover.

Frank Capra, who became well known for his fine directing of *It Happened One Night, Lost Horizon, Arsenic and Old Lace*, and *It's a Wonderful Life*, was born on 18 May 1897 in Bisacquino, Sicily, Italy. He migrated with his family to Los Angeles where he graduated from high school in 1925 and entered the Troop College of Technology (later the California Institute of Technology) to study chemical engineering. 'I discovered poetry at Caltech,' he said. 'Can you imagine that? It was the turning point in my life.' He became successful as a writer for Hal Roach and comedian Harry Langdon who promoted him to director. Married and divorced, he was fired by Langdon and moved on to Columbia Pictures where he earned $3000 a week in 1928. He was also introduced to a young widow, Lucille Warner Reyburn, who became his second wife in 1932, following the affair with Stanwyck. He won Oscars for *Mr Deeds Goes to Washington* (1937) and *You Can't Take It With You* (1938).

Only five feet seven inches tall, Capra was ruggedly handsome with dark piercing eyes and was very charming, but he was not a ladies' man. He was a workaholic who didn't have time for frivolous affairs. His feelings for Barbara were serious and intense, warm and generous.

'She was naive, unsophisticated, caring less about make-up, clothes or hairdo,' Capra wrote about Stanwyck in his memoirs. 'This chorus girl could grab your heart and tear it to pieces. She knew nothing about camera tricks, how to "cheat" her looks so her face could be seen, how to restrict her body movements in close shots. She just turned it on – and everything else on the stage stopped.'

Including his heart. Capra knew about Fay's heavy drinking

and that his jealous obsession with Barbara was causing the marriage to crumble despite her efforts to hold it together. 'I fell in love with Stanwyck,' he said, 'and had I not been more in love with Lucille Reyburn, I would have asked Barbara to marry me after she called it quits with Frank Fay.' Without admitting to an intimate affair with Barbara, Capra said they were very close and that their relationship was vital and important. 'I wish I could tell you more about it,' he wrote, 'but I can't, I shouldn't and I won't, but she was delightful.'

Author Joseph McBride, in his 1992 biography of the director, said that Stanwyck and Capra were lovers for two years and that she was the one who ended the affair, but they would remain close professionally and personally.

CHAPTER FOUR

Triumph

The New York Times headlined their review of *Ladies of Leisure*: 'Miss Stanwyck Triumphs!' *Photoplay Magazine* raved, 'It is really a fine picture because of the tap-dancing beauty who had in her the spirit of a great artist. Her name is Barbara Stanwyck. Go and be amazed by this Barbara girl.'

Ladies of Leisure was one of Stanwyck's greatest achievements and many film historians insist she never did better work. Hollywood opened its arms to her, but the praise did not go to her head. She ignored the social butterflies who sent invitations to their prestigious parties, and the producers and directors who had previously snubbed her had to wait in line.

Fay did not figure on Barbara's overnight recognition when he bargained with Harry Cohn. He was not faring nearly as well. He was meant to ad lib, and he needed laughter and applause to feed his ego. Sadly he was a victim of the transition from silent to talking pictures. *The New York Times* praised his performance in *Bright Lights* (1931), but pointed out that the sound was none too good and the scenes were out of focus. He received fair reviews for *God's Gift to Women* with Joan Blondell and Louise Brooks, but the trend for Fay was downhill. He began negotiating with New York theatre owners for his Broadway return before he fell from grace in Hollywood.

In the meantime, Barbara refused to commit herself, but signed non-exclusive contracts with Columbia Pictures and Warner Brothers. This was a smart choice she made on her own and which set a pattern of independence that was the hallmark of her professional life. This decision had nothing to do with Fay with whom she was still very much in love.

The Hollywood contract players were moulded by their studios and became the great movie stars who remain legends to this day. Stanwyck was one of the very few actresses who did not want to be contractually obligated for seven years to a single studio because she wanted the right to choose her own parts.

Warner Brothers gave her star billing in *Illicit*, a film that was far ahead of its time. Barbara played a girl who prefers living with a man (James Rennie) rather than marrying him. He lures her to the altar where their problems begin.

It's not known how much Fay was earning, but Stanwyck made $1000 a week for *Ladies of Leisure* that took five weeks of filming. Cohn then signed her for three pictures, offering $12,000 for the first one.

After a year in California, Fay managed a limited engagement at the Palace in New York and intended to re-establish his stage career. He told Barbara she could retire from films. 'Remember our agreement,' he said. 'I'm the breadwinner in this family.' Unfortunately she was not in charge of her own destiny any more. Columbia refused to let her accompany Frank to New York because she was contractually committed to do *Ten Cents a Dance*. She pleaded with Harry Cohn to let her go with Fay but he flatly refused because he knew 'that bastard' Frank would deliberately find a way to keep Barbara in New York. She wanted to be with her husband on their second wedding anniversary, but Cohn would not change his mind. She claimed that her marriage came first, but her career was flourishing and this meant security to Stanwyck. Frank was a perfect example of how fickle success can be and it was not to be taken for granted. She had faith in Fay and would stand by him until he was back on his feet again, but this was one of the most difficult times of her life. She would look back and shudder; questioning her good fortune and the cards fate had dealt her. Taking nothing for granted, she worked night and day while Frank complained and drank.

In *Ten Cents a Dance*, Barbara's Brooklyn accent came in handy as a taxi dancer. One of her best lines was in answer to, 'What's a guy gotta do to dance with you?'

'All you need is a ticket and some courage,' she smirks.

The director of *Ten Cents a Dance* was Lionel Barrymore who suffered from severe arthritis. He was taking medication that put him to sleep during most of the filming. Barbara rose above this potential problem and made a comment that he did the best he could under the circumstances. 'I had to try a little harder, that's all,' she said. *Ten Cents a Dance*, co-starring Ricardo Cortez and Sally Blane (Loretta Young's sister), is the title that describes the weak plot. *The New York Times* wrote, '. . . all three of the principals contribute capable performances, with Miss Stanwyck standing out most brightly.'

Barbara went back to Warner Brothers for *Night Nurse* starring a new actor, Clark Gable. 'Joan Blondell and I were in awe of him,' she said. 'When he walked on the set I was in a faint and had to sit down.' There were plenty of punches and violence in the film and Gable, as the bad guy, is involved in most of it.

Hollywood Reporter gave him a good review, but mentioned, 'The best things about this movie are its title and cast names plus the Misses Stanwyck and Blondell stripping two or three times during the picture.' Actually, they were changing clothes, but they weren't too modest about it.

When Fay returned to Hollywood, Warner Brothers informed him they had put his future projects on hold. His last movie, *Bright Lights,* premiered in September 1930 and failed miserably. Barbara's career was gliding along nicely and she was very much in demand, which put a strain on the marriage. Fay moped around in their Malibu beach house while Barbara worked and faced reporters, curious about their relationship, alone. In March 1931 she denied that her marriage was in trouble. 'Frank has turned a lot of things down,' she lied. 'He's considering many offers.' She blamed Warner Brothers for giving him bad scripts and said the same thing could happen to her. 'I'm a star now,' she pointed out, 'but give me two or three bad pictures and Hollywood would consider me a flop again.' Barbara also emphasised that Fay was responsible for her success – how he had rushed her screen test to Frank Capra that resulted in *Ladies of Leisure.* She admitted Fay would prefer it if she didn't work. 'He's old fashioned. He thinks a woman's place is in the home.'

Frank heavy drinking kept him in an ugly mood. By the time Barbara came home each evening, he was drunk and unruly. She knew he belonged in the theatre and, if he were single, could return to New York City and pick up where he left off. Worse, he had to face the fact that everyone in Hollywood knew his wife was rapidly becoming a big star while he was rapidly becoming a has-been and a drunk. Reporters called the Fays at home every day because rumours were flying. One of them wrote that Barbara said she couldn't talk because she was busy baking a cake. 'Hell, she can't even boil water,' a reporter snickered.

Neighbours of the Fays complained to the police about terrible fights, doors slamming at all hours of the night, dishes smashed, voices screaming obscenities and cars screeching in and out of the driveway all night. When police arrived there was nothing they could do but warn the Fays that they were disturbing the peace. These incidents made the newspapers and Barbara laughed them off as silly and exaggerated, but Frank went public when he knocked Barbara down in a nightclub, accusing her of having too much to drink.

Frank Capra persuaded Stanwyck to play a phoney evangelist in *The Miracle Woman,* who falls in love with a blind man (David Manners) and finds God at the finish. The movie was banned in Great Britain for 'irreverence', making it more appealing to the American public. Based thinly on the life of Aimee Semple McPherson, Stanwyck was excellent, but the film was not a success. Capra said *The Miracle Woman* could have been a film classic and blamed himself for its failure. 'I weaselled,' he wrote. 'I insisted on a "heavy" to take the heat off Stanwyck the evangelist. He cons her into it. He gets wealthy. She becomes his flamboyant stooge. Did she or did she not herself believe those "inspiring" sermons delivered in diaphanous robes, with live lions at her side? I don't know. Stanwyck didn't know, and neither did the audience.' *Variety* commented, 'There is no doubt after reviewing this release, picture and theater men will agree that Capra can do more with Barbara Stanwyck than any other director she has worked with.'

And indeed he could because he was still in love with her. 'Divorce that bastard and marry me,' he pleaded with Barbara, who was so torn between him and Fay, she was close to a nervous breakdown. Always for the underdog, she had great compassion for her husband despite their disagreements, and maybe Capra had a chance for lasting happiness with his fiancée Lucille Reyburn, who was getting fed up with his reluctance to get married.

It was too much for Barbara when Capra wanted her to do *Forbidden* with him straight away. She needed a vacation, time out, a chance to think. She did not report for work on 17 July 1931. The reason was money, she said. She had received $16,000 for *The Miracle Woman* and demanded $50,000 to do *Forbidden*. Harry Cohn refused and barred her from working for another studio. Eventually, they compromised and she went back to work.

Stanwyck resumed filming *Forbidden* with Adolph Menjou as the married district attorney and father of her illegitimate daughter. She gives the baby to him and his crippled wife, marries a cad and kills him when he threatens to expose her secret. Her lover pardons her and on his deathbed, leaves half of his estate to her, but she tears up the will and disappears.

Barbara's real life was almost as depressing as the plot of *Forbidden*. During production, she was thrown from a horse and ended up in hospital. Her tailbone had been fractured and both legs were sprained. She would suffer pain from this fall for the rest of her life. A few weeks later, another accident rocked Barbara when the Fays' beach house burned to the ground, taking with it pictures of her childhood. She and Fay settled down in a Brentwood mansion at 441 North Rockingham across the street from Joan Crawford who lived at 426. Frank resumed his heavy drinking and often beat Stanwyck so badly she fled into Joan's arms for comfort.

Capra, meanwhile, went to Europe for a much-needed

vacation to sort out his feelings for Barbara and his fiancée, but Lucille made up his mind for him. She was going to marry someone else, she told him. Stunned, Capra rushed back to her and they were married in New York on 1 February 1932. Barbara sent them a telegram of congratulations.

The New York Times was not enthusiastic about *Forbidden* but praised Stanwyck and Menjou for doing everything possible with the roles. London's *Film Critic* said: 'Miss Stanwyck's emotional scenes with Menjou show that she can hold her own with any actress on the screen today.'

With Capra now married and not pleading for her to leave Fay, Barbara went to New York and shocked her fans and Hollywood by appearing opposite her husband at the Palace. Part of the act was strictly slapstick. All right, the press reported, she was his wife and had been a chorus girl and flapper. But when she did scenes from *Ladies of Leisure*, *The Miracle Woman*, and *Forbidden* on the Palace stage, this was not considered to be in good taste. She drew the crowds, of course, despite Fay's taking all the credit; New York had missed him so much, he said, after Hollywood begged for his talent.

Photoplay reviewed a skit written by Fay: 'Let us draw a kindly, charitable veil over the next ten minutes. It is Christmas in a department store, and Babs has been caught snitching tin soldiers for her "little crippled bovver". Stanwyck labors on – it is like setting Lionel Barrymore to play a conventional English butler named Meadows. And so the afternoon wears paper-thin. Fay holds the stage for half an hour with the aid of assistant buffoons, but it is easy to sense he is not gripping and mowing down the audience as he did when he was Crowned Prince of Seventh Avenue, 'ere the Hollywood goldfields lured him away. And Barbara! She darts on and darts off – displaying the rich

Hollywood wardrobe at Frankie's laughing behest. The bill winds up with a Grand Afterpiece in which the gorgeous one is surrounded by eight clowns, counting Fay, in outlandish states of undress, red noses and fake moustaches. Alas, it is as funny as a plane crash.'

Fay's resentment clouded his ability to think rationally. Not only was he envious of Barbara's popularity, he was now jealous of other men and would not allow her out of his sight. When he was on stage by himself, she was instructed to watch from the wings so he knew her whereabouts. Everyone at the Palace knew Fay was straining to keep his name in lights. Louella Parsons hinted in her newspaper column that all concerned wondered how many more sacrifices Stanwyck would have to make for her husband. Barbara said, 'I would remain with Frank at the Palace indefinitely were it not for my film commitments in Hollywood.'

Stanwyck always pretended to be the happily married lady whose loyalty to her husband was unquestionable, but Fay had good reason to keep an eye on her. Capra was married happily, but now he suspected that his wife had resumed her sexual relationship with Humphrey Bogart, whom she knew intimately in New York during her flapper days. Bogie considered Barbara a very passionate woman who preferred women to men and believed that in her heart she was a lesbian. That was his impression according to Darwin Porter in his book, *Humphrey Bogart: The Early Years*. He got his information from Bogart's friend, actor Kenneth MacKenna. Barbara is quoted as telling Bogie, 'I save my real loving, my gentle side, for women. With men, things immediately revolve around power play.'

Stanwyck was glad to go back to Hollywood, but not happy with *Shopworn*, a low-budget film with a shallow script. Once again she played a girl from the wrong side of the tracks in love with a wealthy gentleman (Regis Toomey) whose socially prominent mother confronts Barbara, who wins her over eventually. *The Times* of London said the movie was dull and characterless, but 'Stanwyck does what she can with a thankless part.' The *New York Herald Tribune* praised her: 'There is something about the straightforward sincerity of Miss Stanwyck which makes everything she does upon the stage or screen seem creditable and rather poignant. But in such antique surroundings, the work of the star is virtually ineffective.'

In her next film, *So Big*, Barbara ages from a young to older woman, a farmer's widow who is a dedicated schoolteacher and devoted to her son 'So Big' (Dickie Moore). The young man leaves home looking for easy money and a good time. In the end, she has faith that his girlfriend (Bette Davis) will make a man out of him.

According to film historian Lawrence Quirk, Davis resented Stanwyck's rapid success, and was difficult during the production of *So Big*. When Bette blew her lines, she said the scene made her jittery. Barbara snapped, 'You make yourself jittery. Try to fit into things!' Davis was furious and tried to steal as many scenes from Barbara as possible.

'She's an egotistical little bitch!' Stanwyck told director William Wellman.

So Big received mixed reviews. *The New York Times* thought Barbara was unsuited to the role, but said 'Bette Davis is unusually competent.'

The *New York World Telegram* said, 'By her performance in *So Big*, Barbara Stanwyck definitely establishes herself with this writer as being a brilliant emotional actress. No matter what one might think about the picture, the final conviction of anyone who sees Miss Stanwyck's Miss Peake will be that she herself contributes a fine and stirring performance, making it a characterization which is direct and eloquent all the way.'

In 1932, the American people were slowly emerging from the Great Depression that had affected most industries, but not the movie business.

The public turned to Hollywood for a few hours of entertainment to unburden themselves from the dreary reality of life and they managed to scrape up ten cents at the box office. Musicals were popular, of course, but tear jerkers drew an audience, too. Rather than cry alone, they were drawn to shed tears with Barbara Stanwyck in *The Purchase Price*, the story of a girl running away from her gangster boyfriend and becoming a mail-order bride of a farmer (George Brent). As in most of her films, Barbara's wicked past catches up with her and there are tense minutes before a happy ending.

The outlook of Stanwyck's marriage was not as rosy. She began sinking to Fay's level by keeping up with him drink for drink. He blamed her for their disagreements and lack of friends in Hollywood. Gradually they were being excluded from parties and not invited to join the usual crowds at nightclubs. Barbara wasn't fazed because she was too busy studying scripts in the evenings and on her days off. But Fay was losing all of his important contacts in show business and he needed to mingle socially. He was arrested for drunken driving and hit-and-run when his car hit another on Beverly Boulevard, but charges were dropped when witnesses refused to testify.

Barbara could never repay Fay for making her movie career possible, but she would try, and after hours of sober discussions, they decided to write, produce and star in their own Broadway revue. While Barbara did four films in succession, Fay was busy writing *Tattle Tales*.

CHAPTER FIVE

Goodbye Faysie

Frank Capra thought Barbara deserved an Oscar and chose an 'art' film, *The Bitter Tea of General Yen*, to attract attention to her versatile talents. Despite his artful direction, Barbara was not convincing as the American mistress of a Chinese warlord (Nils Asther). Her fans wondered why she bothered with it, and critics agreed. *The New York Times* said, 'Her powerful voice is scarcely what is needed to carry out the theme of this tale of romance between a handsome Chinese general and a lovely American missionary.'

In *Ladies They Talk About*, Stanwyck was a wisecracking bank bandit who is reformed by Preston Foster. This film was made in only 24 hours and received mixed reviews.

'I guess everyone in Hollywood is glamorous but me,' Barbara said in 1933. 'So I accepted a role in *Baby Face* strictly for the glamor and hated it.' Co-starring George Brent, Barbara, as Lily Powers, uses her wiles as a beautiful woman to get whatever – and whomever – she wants. The movie opens with Lily being abused by her father who uses her as a prostitute. It was a film ahead of its time and rushed to theatres before a revised Production Code went into effect. *The New York Times* wrote, '*Baby Face*, the film that recently aroused the ire of Will Hays, who's in charge of censoring films, and also responsible for the resignation of Darryl Zanuck as assistant to Jack Warner, is now on exhibition at the Strand. It is an unsavory subject, with incidents set forth in an inexpert fashion.' The critics were more interested in the leading character – a whore – than in reviewing Barbara's performance. As a result of the Hays Code, a man and woman were not allowed in the same bed, and kisses were limited to three seconds.

Barbara got more sleaze than glamour in *Baby Face* and she knew exactly what she was doing, sitting in on script revises and offering suggestions. *Variety* summed up the film: 'Any hotter than this for public showing would call for an asbestos audience blanket.'

Ever in My Heart followed quickly. In this mediocre film she plays an American woman who marries a German officer, finds out he is a spy and puts poison in their wine. Dramatically, she waits for him to die before committing suicide.

Stanwyck invested $125,000 in *Tattle Tales*, Fay's stage revue that played major cities while gearing up for the Broadhurst Theater in New York on 11 June 1933. It closed after 28 days. One critic summed up the disaster, 'Frank Fay does not know where to draw the line. I like Fay very much and I always have, but he refuses to believe that there is a difference between acting and being Frank Fay. He will be what nature made him, the chips fall where they may. He is a problem child. Now at the 44th Street Theatre he is producing a vaudeville show and he is one of its three stars. The trouble with it is he thinks he owns it! . . . There is no one there to stop him from doing what he wants. So he does everything and anything he wants all evening. If he is funny for a minute he jumps to the childish conclusion that if he keeps going for ten minutes he will be ten times as funny. He never knows when to go home.

'There ought to be a commission appointed for the conservation of Frank Fay. Or he could go to a good psychiatrist and be turned into an artist with hardly any trouble at all.

'I hate to see Frank Fay go to waste. He is too good.'

Barbara lost her investment and Fay was losing his battle with the bottle. She could think of only one other solution to their marital problems, but she could not have children due to at least one botched abortion when she was a chorus girl. According to Joan Crawford, they both suffered the same fate. 'Most abortions were dangerous in those days. Botched is a nice way of putting it,' Joan said. 'Birth control was almost nonexistent.'

Frank wanted a child of his own who – he thought – would inherit his talent and genius. Since that wasn't possible they adopted a 10-month-old baby in December 1932 from the Children's Home Society and christened him Dion Anthony. The Fays 'played house' for a few weeks and then hired a series of nannies to take over. Barbara said it would be wonderful to adopt a lot of kids because she was an orphan and knew what it was like to not have a home. Unfortunately, she had no conception of what motherhood entailed. It was all an act and a pathetic one. She should have thought long and hard about adopting a child. Did she expect her maternal instincts to blossom into her becoming Catherine Stevens, who sacrificed everything for her babies? Unwisely Barbara did not take the time to consider the responsibilities of raising a child. What were the boy's chances growing up with a uninterested, working mother and an alcoholic father?

Dion got to know his nanny very well because Barbara was at the studio all day and, in the evening, if she wasn't learning her lines for the morning, the Fays were nightclubbing. In later years Dion said the only attention he got from his mother was when she scolded him and if photographers were allowed in the house to take pictures. When friends dropped by, Barbara didn't want to be bothered with him.

A neighbour recalled, 'We seldom saw the boy after his father threw him in the swimming pool. Unfortunately, things were getting worse in that house. We hated to call the police, but enough is enough!'

Gossip columnists hinted that the Fay marriage was over, but Barbara fought back as usual. 'Sometimes it seems that Hollywood does not want people to be happy,' she said. 'Why don't they leave us alone? We're going to be happy despite everyone. They are determined that nobody has a private life that is immune from chatter and scandal. You know that people are watching you all the time, looking for the slightest thing to gossip about and, if they don't find it, they make it up. That is why Frank and I go out with only close friends. All we ask is to be allowed to live in peace, but some people resent this. Well, they'll just have to go on resenting.'

But one night at the Trocadero nightclub in Hollywood, the Fays got into a royal battle and he landed a wallop to her chin that sent her to the floor. After a brief parting Barbara was the first to break the silence with a letter:

No need to tell you that I felt blue when you left. I can't stand your being unhappy in any way at all. Whatever you want to do I am with you 100 percent, only I do not want you to sacrifice yourself in any way. I can live any place or go anywhere with you. I love you just as much as it is possible for a woman to love a man. If I were born with anything fine in me, and I choose to think I was, from what I know of my father and mother, you have brought that fineness to the surface.

I cannot imagine life without you and I'm not being melodramatic. I probably do not give you that impression at any time – that of not being able to imagine life without you, I mean. However, that is due to my lack of education and not being able to express myself clearly in speech.

I can write it, however. You are always right about everything so you must be right about what you want to do. Please, Frank, love me – whatever you do, and wherever you go, take me. For there I shall be content.

The Fays reconciled and Frank was offered a small part in Warner Brothers' picture, *Stars Over Broadway* with Pat O'Brien, James Melton (his film debut) and Jane Froman. Fay received eighth billing in his last attempt at a comeback in films and, once again, took this setback out on his wife by calling Jack Warner to complain about Barbara's working hours. 'She leaves before dawn and doesn't get home until after dark,' Frank bellowed. Warner let her go, but she was consistent in press interviews that Hollywood gossip was responsible for her marital difficulties.

The Fays, however, did all right at destroying their marriage by themselves. Sitting around the swimming pool one afternoon in 1934, they fought bitterly because Barbara had gone to a burlesque show. Frank struck her again and she hit the ground. Dion burst into tears, and Barbara threatened divorce.

The Stanwyck myth is far removed from that of the 27-year-old ex-chorus girl weeping for her husband's return. He was, despite his drunken brawls and waning career, the stronger of the two. She paid the bills but he was master of the house. It would take time before she had enough faith in herself to stand alone and put the past in perspective.

Frank would have regained his professional status had she not sought him out after each separation. In a letter dated 17 November 1934, she wrote to him on his birthday:

> Dear Kid,
>
> I haven't diamonds, no watch, no nothing. I feel rather funny not giving you anything, but it just has to be. And so, Frank, all I have to give you today is my prayers that all goes well with you. And whatever you do shall be right, and that God will keep your path well lighted so that you will never hurt yourself. God bless you and spare you.
>
> BarBara

Three days later Willard Mack died suddenly of a heart attack in Los Angeles at the age of 57. Mack had been gravitating between Hollywood and New York as a successful writer and director.

Barbara was shattered. The timing made it worse for her, losing the two most influential men in her life at the same time. Mack's death came as such a shock, it changed her way of thinking. 'I'll never divorce Frank Fay,' she told reporters. 'You can gossip all you want, but if I can't stay married, I'll get out of pictures!' But Fay went on a drunken rampage in 1935. He insulted Barbara in public, continued to pick fights at parties while raving to the press that he was the star in the family and his wife was going to retire. Reporters could recite his speeches by heart.

In August, the Fays came very close to killing each other

during a brutal battle at home. Stanwyck fled over the surrounding wall with Dion and took refuge at Joan Crawford's house. Trembling with fear, Barbara wept, 'This is the end. I can't take it any longer. I'm never going back to that house!'

'What about your collection of antiques and silver?' Joan asked.

Barbara shrugged. 'Things that used to mean so much to me aren't important any more.'

'You're a goddam fool not to take what belongs to you!'

'I saved my most precious possession,' Barbara said.

'What's that?'

'My life.'

Barbara filed for divorce immediately.

On 31 December 1935, Barbara and Frank signed a pre-divorce agreement, giving her custody of Dion and Frank visiting rights twice a week. She was granted the house in Brentwood, but sold it for $80,000 and moved into a ranch in the Northridge section of the San Fernando Valley near her agent, Zeppo Marx, the youngest of the famous brothers, and his wife Marion. Here she established Marwyck (Marx Stanwyck) Ranch to breed thoroughbred horses on 140 acres of land, and she offered Uncle Buck a home to help her with the ranch.

Earning $100,000 a picture, Stanwyck did not ask for alimony.

During the tumultuous pre-divorce months of 1934 and 1935, Barbara managed to keep her name on movie marquees, and critics usually applauded her for rescuing these consequential films. She would co-star with Joel McCrea in six pictures, the first of which was *Gambling Lady* for Warner Brothers. In the title role she falls in love with another gambler and gets involved in murder.

In First National's *A Lost Lady*, Stanwyck played a woman

married to an older man (Frank Morgan). Plans to run away with her lover (Ricardo Cortez) are aborted when she decides to stay with her sick husband.

The Secret Bride (Warner Brothers) was a homicide melodrama, with Barbara playing a governor's daughter who keeps her marriage to an attorney-general (Warren Wiliam) a secret to save her father from impeachment.

First National's *The Woman in Red* is typical Stanwyck. She married a socialite (Gene Raymond) and is snubbed by his family and friends.

Red Salute for United Artists was Barbara's first comedy role. She plays a college girl who leans towards Communism until she falls in love with an American soldier (Robert Young).

Finally, in 1935, at the height of her domestic problems with Frank Fay, Stanwyck got the plum role of *Annie Oakley*, directed by George Stevens for RKO. Annie, 'the rifle lady' of Buffalo Bill's wild west shows falls in love with an insolent star shooter (Preston Foster) and deliberately misses her target because 'he's so pretty'. *Annie Oakley* was hailed by critics as 'superior entertainment'. *The New York Times* thought it was Stanwyck's most striking performance in a long time.

Her next 20th Century-Fox (1936) film rivals *Mexicali Rose* as one of Stanwyck's worst – *A Message to Garcia* co-starring John Boles. The message came from President McKinley in 1898 to Cuban leader, General Garcia, enlisting his help in the war against Spain. The *New York Evening Post* critic said it all: 'It bothers us that Barbara, cast as a Cuban senorita should talk perfect Brooklyn.' *The New York Times* wrote that it was 'as undocumented a piece of historical claptrap as the film city has produced.'

In the same year, Barbara did *The Bride Walks Out* for RKO – the story about a married couple struggling to make ends meet because the husband (Gene Raymond) does not want his wife going to work. The film has just enough slapstick to make it good fun.

Unlike her friend, Joan Crawford, who shed her first husband Douglas Fairbanks Jr as she would an old fur coat, Stanwyck walked into the divorce court feeling inferior and depressed. She told the judge that too many women were attracted to Fay and he enjoyed it too much. Afterwards, she remarked to reporters, 'I hated to have to do this but it seems the only salvation for both of us. Frank is better off alone and so am I. I want our divorce to be free of bitterness.'

Fay forged ahead with nightclub engagements. 'I should've done this before,' he said, 'but I believed a husband and wife should live together. Barbara made it big in Hollywood. I helped when I had pull at Warners and they gave her a break. I'm not sorry I did this, but who the hell could've predicted the outcome. There is no way out in the end except divorce.'

But Barbara was making it difficult for him to see Dion. 'I'm not always in California,' Frank complained, 'but called as often as possible. For a hundred bucks a call, all I got was "Hello, Daddy" and dead air. When I got to town I wasn't allowed to see my son.' Barbara told her lawyers that Frank was always drunk and, therefore, dangerous to the welfare of the child. When he was barred from the ranch, a judge ordered Barbara to allow him to see Dion. She refused and was summoned to court to give valid reasons why Frank could not exercise his rights.

While lawyers for both sides prepared for court, Barbara dated handsome actor George Brent who hasn't received adequate credit for his great sex appeal. He married five times and was involved with Joan Crawford, Greta Garbo, Kay Francis, Marlene Dietrich and Bette Davis.

Brent had several things in common with Barbara. He was Irish, orphaned in his youth and began his career on the stage. Their affair was brief, however, because Stanwyck had not got Fay out of her system yet. 'I'm not interested in romance,' she said. 'Right now I have everything I want. I've given up wishing.'

But in the fall of 1936, every girl's wish walked into her arms. Without looking or searching, little Ruby Stevens from Brooklyn found Camelot.

CHAPTER SIX

Bob

Zeppo and Marion Marx arranged a blind date for Barbara at the Trocadero nightclub. When she arrived there was no one sitting at the reserved table other than MGM's matinee idol, Robert Taylor, whom she recognised. They chatted politely, but each time the door opened, she looked around. Feeling a bit uncomfortable, he asked her to dance.

'I can't right now,' she said. 'I'm waiting for someone – a Mr Artique.'

'Mr Artique?' Taylor frowned. 'Never heard of him. What's the first name?'

'I don't know,' she said, keeping her eye on the door.

'That's a peculiar name.'

'Maybe I'm not pronouncing it right, but it's close enough.'

'Artique . . . Artique . . .' he repeated. Then he laughed. 'That's me! R.T. Get it?'

Taylor was more excited about solving the puzzle than she was. Despite his enthusiasm over a date with the distinguished actress, he was still in love with starlet Irene Hervey, but watching Bob and Barbara on the dance floor that night at the Trocadero, no one would believe that each carried a torch for someone else.

Having been married to an egotist, Stanwyck considered Taylor very refreshing in a town of phonies. His face was perfect. Beautiful, in fact, but he had not lost his Midwest innocence. His hair was black and his eyes were blue and he had a widow's peak. He was polite, attentive, youthfully charming – and in awe of Barbara who was touched by his admiration and lack of pretence. It was, quite simply, a delightful evening shared by two people who were poles apart. Bob sent a dozen long-stemmed roses the following day, thanking her for a wonderful evening. She had gotten flowers from men before, but had never known a courtship like this one. Bob invited her and Dion to the Santa Monica pier where they enjoyed the amusement park, walked on the boardwalk, and were so informal, they blended into the crowd. Barbara felt like a teenager and might have laughed at the simplicity of it all, but Taylor, who was unpretentious, attentive and refreshing, enchanted her. Joan Crawford invited them to her home where they could relax and avoid reporters and fans, and the couple spent quiet evenings at home with Marion and Zeppo. Neither Bob nor Barbara wanted to be seen together in public since she was involved in a messy court action and Taylor had his obligation to Metro-Goldwyn-Mayer as a single, unattached male idol who was expected to date young starlets. Barbara Stanwyck was four years older and divorced – not the type suited to his clean-cut, all-American-boy image. Irene Hervey had been perfect for him, but MGM refused to allow them to marry. He was more desirable to the female moviegoer if he remained single.

'I wanted to get married,' Hervey said. 'I could have waited but Allan Jones proposed and I accepted because I thought he had more potential than Bob. Allan and I were married for 21 years and I never regretted my decision.' Their son Jack Jones inherited his father's great singing voice and became a favourite on television, in nightclub circuits and Las Vegas.

Robert Taylor was born Spangler Arlington Brugh in Filley, Nebraska, on 5 August 1911. He grew up in nearby Beatrice. His father was a country doctor and his mother a sickly woman who was not expected to survive her son's birth.

Arly, as he was known, wanted to be a concert cellist, and rode his horse Gypsy to Doane College for lessons. 'Professor Grey was my inspiration,' Taylor said. 'I enrolled at Doane to study with him and was lost when the professor told me he was accepting a teaching job at Pomona College in Claremont, California. My whole world fell apart.'

Looking back, Taylor didn't know how he persuaded his parents to let him transfer to Pomona. 'It was a miracle,' he said, 'and even more astounding that my old car made it all the way to California.'

Grey was very strict and he objected to Arly taking up debating, which led to his being asked to join the Drama Club. Grey said this was not dedication to the cello, but Arly explained, 'I was a member of the debating team in high school and did some acting, too.' Though he kept the cello for the rest of his life, he turned to acting and got the lead as Captain Stanhope in R.C. Sheriff's powerful play *Journey's End*. With the help of Pomona alumni, actor Joel McCrea, Arly got a screen test at Metro-Goldwyn-Mayer for a crime short with Virginia Bruce, but heard nothing. Shortly after his graduation the following year, Dr Brugh died and Arly's mother moved to California and set up housekeeping for her son.

In February 1934 MGM finally recognised Arly and signed

him to a seven-year contract paying only 35 dollars a week, making Brugh the lowest-paid actor or actress in the history of Hollywood. 'My father did not have much money when he died,' Brugh said. 'There were a lot of patients who didn't pay him and he didn't try to collect the funds, so my mother and I had to live on what I earned. Even in 1934, 35 dollars a week didn't go very far. Then they changed my name to Robert Taylor. Who could accept a name like that after being Spangler Arlington Brugh?'

But with a salary he couldn't live on, and a name he hated, Bob stuck it out. In his eighth film, *Magnificent Obsession*, with Irene Dunne in 1935 he became a star and was earning $750 a week.

If it's true that opposites attract, Taylor and Stanwyck are the classic example. He was still a kid when they met, while she had never really been a child. He was a box-office attraction. She was an actress. Taylor was well educated, Barbara was not. He was gentle. She was tough. He loved the country, she could only breathe in the city. He liked women in frilly dresses and soft colours. She wore tailored clothes made out of men's materials. He treated a woman like a lady. Barbara lit her own cigarettes and opened doors for herself. Bob was discreet. She was brutally frank. He enjoyed hunting. Barbara thought it was cruel. Bob collected rifles. She was terrified of guns.

Taylor was an inexperienced lover.

Barbara had been around.

Bob's understatement to the press was that, 'Miss Stanwyck is not the sort of woman I would have met in Nebraska.'

Reporters got a snicker out of that one.

Years later Taylor said, 'Barbara taught me everything I know.'

Barbara and Bob stayed away from nightclubs to avoid

publicity, but they attended the same parties. If one was invited, the other was also. Otherwise neither showed up. Their names were linked in the gossip columns and occasionally a picture of the couple appeared in newspapers. MGM was not concerned just yet. They reversed their professional outlook and decided to exploit Taylor's relationship with a woman, though they did not want him engaged or married. They signed Stanwyck to co-star with Bob in *His Brother's Wife*, her first picture at MGM. It was a limp film with Taylor as a scientist who chooses his research over her. For revenge she marries his brother, but eventually follows him into the jungle and proves her faith in him by injecting herself with spotted fever germs and is saved by his serum.

The New York Times summed up the critical consensus: 'Whatever else may be said of it, there is no disputing the formulary perfection of the Capitol Theater's latest gift from MGM. Incredibly romantic, glossily produced, expertly directed and peopled by the sort of players most often encountered on the covers of fan magazines, *His Brother's Wife* – even to its title – has been so astutely aimed at the box office that we can but stiffen resignedly and wait for the marker to cry bull's eye. A triumph of machine made art, it is a picture that will succeed no matter how we, in our ivory tower, rail against it for its romantic absurdity.'

Taylor was more excited about *Private Number* because he got top billing over his leading lady, Loretta Young. Bob had never seen his name in lights above all the others. 'Don't let it go to your head,' Barbara told him. 'Loretta's been at it for years to get her name up there, buster. You've been at it a short time. The trick is to keep it there.'

Taylor said, 'That was the best advice I ever had.'

MGM mogul Louis B. Mayer knew that Bob's mother was a religious fanatic, who made a habit of reminding him about the sins and evils in Hollywood. She was a nuisance rather than the supporting figure he needed. Mayer hoped Stanwyck would be a mother-substitute and give Taylor the confidence and encouragement he needed. Although she was only four years older than him, she was older than her years.

The MGM contract players were Mayer's 'family', and he made it his business to know everything that transpired in their personal lives to protect them from scandal. He was not above blackmail if there was no alternative. He threatened to destroy Joan Crawford and Clark Gable in 1933 if they did not break off their love affair. Both were married and had yet to establish themselves. With one phone call, Mayer could have prevented them from ever working again in Hollywood. He forced his gay actors, such as Van Johnson, to get married. He arranged for Van's close friends, Edie and Keenan Wynn to divorce so Van could marry Edie and have children. The public assumed homosexuals and lesbians did not get married, but they often did to protect their images. Louis B. Mayer was the master of manufacturing 'more stars than there were in heaven'. His idea of the perfect contract player was Robert Taylor, a handsome guy from the Midwest, who did what he was told and never complained.

When Stanwyck became involved with Bob, she had to abide by the same rules as he did or walk away. She managed this by keeping her mouth shut.

Banjo on My Knee with Joel McCrea at 20th Century Fox was a light comedy about a bride deserted on her wedding day and forced to entertain for a living. In it, Barbara made her singing debut with Tony Martin and Buddy Ebsen.

At RKO Barbara co-starred with Preston Foster in *The Plough and the Stars* about the 1916 Easter Rebellion in Dublin and its impact on a young married couple.

In 1937, Stanwyck and McCrea teamed up again in the first Dr Kildare movie, *Interns Can't Take Money*, a Paramount release. As the honest and sympathetic Dr Kildare, McCrea received most of the attention and applause.

In Stanwyck's private life, she allowed Taylor to get all the attention and applause. If they were together, she stayed in the background and observed the stampede of female fans who always gathered wherever he was. Barbara's press agent Helen Ferguson said, 'Everyone in Hollywood knew about the affair, but it was publicised as casual dating. Barbara was trying to settle her legal battles with Frank Fay out of court, and MGM was giving Bob the star build-up. Aside from the obvious reasons, Bob and Barbara did not know how they felt about each other. When they realised it was love, they became a steady couple, but there was not a hint of marriage. Mr Mayer made sure of that.'

MGM did, however, exploit their relationship by loaning Taylor to 20th Century Fox for *This Is My Affair* with Stanwyck in 1936. The title was deliberately misleading to lure moviegoers and it worked. The 'affair' was Taylor's undercover job to crush a wave of bank robberies during Theodore Roosevelt's presidency, but the film was a hit. One critic mused, 'Mr Taylor makes love to Miss Stanwyck persuasively.'

Bob had just finished *Camille* with Greta Garbo, but his powdered-down look prompted the press to nickname him 'Pretty Boy' and rumours spread that he was a homosexual – one reason MGM finally allowed him to have an open relationship with Barbara. Reporters harassed Bob and in one spontaneous interview he snarled, 'Ask me anything except about Barbara Stanwyck or if I have hair on my chest!' He spoke to Mayer who advised him to be patient.

CHAPTER SEVEN

Stella

Seldom did Stanwyck want a role as desperately as *Stella Dallas*. She asked Joe McCrea to mention it to his boss, producer Sam Goldwyn. King Vidor, who was directing the film, wanted Stanwyck from the start, but Goldwyn wasn't interested in her. He didn't think she was the type to play the part of a devoted mother who sacrifices everything for her daughter. McCrea and Vidor put pressure on Goldwyn until he agreed to test her. Barbara went through the roof. Why should an actress of her magnitude have to stoop to do a screen test? 'Goldwyn didn't want me, period,' she said. 'I must admit he was frank. He said I wasn't capable. I was too young and I hadn't had enough experience with children. But I tested and he gave me the part.

'The role of Stella was a double challenge because she was two separate women. On the surface she was loud and flamboyant with a touch of vulgarity, but beneath the surface she was fine, heart-warming and noble. Part of her tragedy was that while she recognised her own shortcomings, she was unable to live up to the standards she so painstakingly set for herself.'

The story of *Stella Dallas* is the study of a mother's love and sacrifice. Her ambitions for her daughter, Laurel, were great and yet unselfish – so much so that Stella has to cut herself out of her child's life completely because she's an embarrassment. She married above her class and could not adjust. She wore heavy make-up and gaudy clothes, used vulgar language and lacked social graces. When she realises why people are laughing and staring at her, Stella deliberately plans an affront that freed Laurel of any obligations.

It is ironic that in 1937 Stanwyck would play the sensitive role of a mother willing to make every sacrifice for her child while she was preparing to send her six-year-old adopted son away to school and out of her life. Dion, who was chubby and wore glasses, had not lived up to Barbara's expectations. She did not have the time or patience to be bothered with him.

Sam Goldwyn asked Barbara before giving her the part of Stella, 'How can you "feel" this part? Have you ever suffered over a child?'

'No,' she replied, 'but I can imagine how it would be.'

But unfortunately, she had no conception of what it was like to feel this in reality. If she had put forth one ounce of the energy and devotion into bringing up her son that she put into the character of Stella, she might have succeeded as a mother. Barbara's close friend and press agent Helen Ferguson said, 'Dion was the innocent victim of Barbara's attempt to save her marriage to Frank Fay. Having children is not the way to do that, but she was willing to try anything. She didn't abandon Dion. She sent him away to school because she couldn't devote the time to him that a mother should.'

The New York Times echoed what other critics had to say about *Stella Dallas*: 'Miss Stanwyck's portrayal is as courageous as it is fine. Ignoring the flattery of make-up, she plays Stella as author Olive Higgins Prouty drew her: coarse, cheap, common, given to sleazy dresses, to undulations in her walk, to fatty degeneration of the profile. And yet magnificent as a mother.'

One of Stanwyck's greatest triumphs was her nomination for Best Actress by Motion Picture Academy of Arts and Sciences for her portrayal of Stella.

Robert Taylor bought property next to Barbara's in Northridge, in the far corner of the San Fernando Valley, and 15 miles from the MGM studios. He built a house and stables within walking distance of Marwyck. Fan magazines featured articles about Bob running over to Barbara's for a swim in her pool, or Barbara hopping over to Bob's for dinner. They were seen riding his quarter horses together at sunset, though she was not known for her ability on horseback.

In the spring of 1937, MGM decided to make *A Yank at Oxford* in England to protect its British franchise. It would be the first Hollywood movie to be filmed in Europe. Mayer chose Taylor to play the rugged, cocky Yank in a supreme effort to change his image. Bob was thrilled over the movie, but not over leaving Barbara. He wanted her to promise she would visit him. To be separated for six months is a long time. 'We'll see,' she said in a motherly fashion. 'You'll be busy and so will I. Besides, your house isn't finished. Who's going to oversee everything if I don't?'

Barbara had every reason to be concerned about Bob's trip to England. She wasn't worried about his co-stars Maureen O'Sullivan, happily married to director John Farrow, or Vivien Leigh who was hopelessly in love with Laurence Olivier. But wherever Taylor went, women followed and he was still naive at 26, having been pampered and protected by MGM. The big question was: would he enjoy his freedom in England and not want to be tied down when he returned?

Barbara was not one to fret if she had no control over the situation. Having been hurt so badly by Fay, she was not about to get seriously involved with any man so soon after her heart was broken. Her one salvation was work and she delved into it when Taylor boarded the *Berengaria* for England. Barbara chuckled at the headlines: 'PUBLIC HEART THROB SAILS TODAY. DON'T CRY GIRLS, HE'LL BE BACK!' When the ship docked in Southampton, 5,000 people were on hand to greet him and he had to be smuggled out in a goods lift. The Queen of England said it was a trifle quiet around Buckingham Palace with Robert Taylor getting all the attention. Bob called his 'Queen' in California, and told her the English people were wonderful, even the reporters. Then he proposed marriage again but Barbara prudently said they should wait and agreed six months was a long time to be apart, but suggested he concentrate on doing the one film that would change his image and relieve him once and for all of the abuse he was getting from the American press. She also reminded him that *A Yank at Oxford* was the first American movie to be filmed in Denham Studios and that Hollywood studios were following developments closely, for this could be the beginning of American actors going abroad to face the camera.

Bob loved England and England loved Robert Taylor and, for many years after, he was remembered there as the American movie star who crossed the Atlantic to do a movie in their country. With the MGM brass to keep him company, Bob soon relaxed and got in shape for the rigours of *A Yank at Oxford* about a brash young American coping with English university life. As Lee Sheridan he surprised his fellow students by excelling at track and rowing in the bumper races, but as Robert Taylor he shocked every male from Texas to Tibet with his fine physique. Paris was the first to announce the 'hairy' news. They published a picture of Taylor in athletic trunks and shirt. Underneath his photos, dated 28 August 1937, they printed, '*Mon Dieu, Quel Homme!*'

The American press announced: 'ROBERT TAYLOR BARES CHEST TO PROVE HE-NESS!'

Stanwyck talked to Bob on the phone every day and he never failed to ask her to take the next ship leaving for Europe. She was terrified of flying so that was not an option. When reporters caught up with her, she said, 'I am not going to England to see Bob. He told me yesterday that the weather was not good and filming was being delayed because of rain and he might not be home for Christmas.

'We have no plans for marriage and I have no intention of visiting Bob in England. Can you imagine what would happen if I went? It's bad enough here with you reporters. We wouldn't have a moment's peace. Our transatlantic telephone conversations will have to do for now.'

Cables went back and forth and telephone bills mounted as Bob and Barbara continued their romance miles apart. There were days he felt terribly lonely. 'And on one of those hopeless dreary days,' he said, 'I asked her to marry me. She gave me some flimsy excuses and I hung up in a huff.' Barbara told her agent Helen Ferguson he was still growing up and perhaps shouldn't be tied down. She wanted him to experience fame and fortune. 'Then he will have a better sense of values and will be able to judge what is best for him.'

Actually it was MGM who was Bob's judge and Barbara knew it. They would not have allowed him to get married but unlike Irene Hervey, Barbara was willing to wait. She had very little spare time on her hands, anyway. She went to work in the rousing comedy *Breakfast for Two* at RKO. 'I couldn't possibly have followed *Stella Dallas* with another emotional role,' she said. Stanwyck plays a Texas heiress who tried to make a man out of a rich playboy (Herbert Marshall). The movie borrowed some old lines and gags from silent films that included the cake-in-the-face routine. For Barbara, *Breakfast for Two* was recreation, but when *Stella Dallas* was released in August 1937, she thought about her image as an actress and decided against doing more silly screen farces. She had contracts with RKO and 20th Century Fox, but turned down every script submitted to her. As a result, she was suspended by both studios. 'If you feel strongly enough, you should have the courage of your convictions to carry it through . . . a lot of times a studio knows better than a star whether or not a picture will be a success, but I have to go on my instincts. Sometimes I've been wrong, but more often I've been right,' she commented.

Stanwyck wanted the lead in *Jezebel* very much. She spoke to Jack Warner about it and offered to do a test, but he had no intention of giving the part to anyone other than Bette Davis.

On 14 December 1937, Taylor returned to New York on the *Queen Mary*. Reporters, who taunted and teased him by asking if he had any hair on his legs, bombarded him. When he blurted out, 'Goddam!' MGM publicists stepped in. One newsman came to Bob's defence in an article entitled, THE PRESS AND MR TAYLOR: 'Our sympathies go out to Mr Robert Taylor, the young personable motion picture actor, for being forced again to submit to the severe questionings, not to say heckling, on whether he regards himself as beautiful . . . It used to be big news when Stanley found Livingstone, when a crown Prince was born, or when a great economic or political upheaval shook the world. Today's news is whether Mr Taylor thinks he is beautiful and just how he feels, if at all, about Barbara Stanwyck!'

Bob arrived in Los Angeles laden with gifts for Barbara and

Dion. He made one more attempt to persuade her they should get married. She insisted they wait, but agreed to a secret engagement, pacifying him for the time being. Aside from his obligation to MGM, Barbara explained that Frank Fay had obtained a court order to see their son. 'And you have been mentioned as consort,' she told him. 'It will be messy, but I'll fight him all the way.'

On 17 December 1937, Barbara went on the stand to deny Frank's allegations that Robert Taylor was involved. She insisted Fay was not in his right mind, that he struck her on more than one occasion, and on a drunken spree he threw Dion into the swimming pool.

Fay's attorney asked her, 'Isn't the reason you are barring Mr Fay from visiting his child is because you want the boy to become accustomed to someone else – say Robert Taylor, for instance?'

Stiffening in the witness chair, Barbara answered, 'No.'

'Wasn't it a fact that you were having Mr Taylor to your house frequently so that the child could forget Mr Fay?'

'Mr Taylor was at the house frequently, but it was not so the boy would forget his father.'

'Did not Mr Taylor give the boy gifts on numerous occasions?'

Barbara said that was true. She was then asked about a cheque for 50 dollars that had apparently been made out to the child and signed by Robert Taylor. The judge made the attorney withdraw the question. 'I don't care how many times Mr Taylor came to her home. This is her personal life and has nothing to do with this proceeding.'

On 16 January 1938, Barbara went back on the stand and said she demanded psychiatric examination of Frank Fay. She portrayed him as a man who mingled prayers with profanity, and she submitted 10 affidavits in her attempt to show Fay to be of 'unsound mind'. She then described his peculiar habits. 'When he passed a church, Frank would remove his hands from the wheel of a car and pray, endangering the lives of others.' Fay got into a fistfight with the late Ted Healy, but had to stop to search for his false teeth when Healy knocked them out. Once at the Trocadero, she continued, Fay accused her of drinking too much champagne and knocked her down.

'He's an unfit guardian for the child,' she insisted. 'He drinks too much. He fell into Dion's crib once and fell asleep keeping the boy awake with his snoring. As far as I'm concerned he loves his new store teeth more than his son!'

Stanwyck was asked if it was true she owned 50 racehorses and she gave an affirmative answer.

'Is it true you spent most of Christmas Day at the races instead of at home with your child?' Fay's attorney wanted to know.

Barbara lowered her head and nodded.

Two days later the front-page headlines of every newspaper blared the outcome: TAYLOR CITED. FIGHT IS LOST BY STANWYCK. 'Robert Taylor's name was dragged into the Frank Fay–Barbara Stanwyck custody fight today when attorneys for Fay attempted to cast the Number One Heart Throb of the Screen in the role of a villain in the Santa Claus suit.'

The judge ruled in favour of Fay who would be allowed to visit his son twice a week and on alternate Saturdays, provided he was completely sober and always in the company of the child's nurse, who would be obliged to report his conduct to Stanwyck.

Barbara told her lawyers to appeal because her ex-husband was an 'all-time drunk'.

The bitter court battle for custody rights to Dion was

apparently only a revengeful tug-of-war between Barbara and Frank with no genuine concern for the boy. She wanted Fay out of her life completely and he, in turn, took advantage of his visitation rights to annoy Barbara. When eventually she stopped fighting him, Frank became bored and stopped seeing Dion.

'Above everything,' Stanwyck told the press, 'I want my son to be happy. He needs a sense of security in the home, something I did not have as a child. I can't let him be thrown about like a piece of meat. He needs confidence and courage and love. But I don't want him to be one of the spoiled movie children so I'm sending him to a military school in the near future.'

Though Barbara admitted she was at the racetrack, she appeared in a fan magazine article about the very special cosy Christmas she was planning for her little boy. The tree and the presents and the decorations, all to make him feel that he belonged. She would protect him like a mother should, tuck him in at bedtime and be there when he cried at night. 'There's nothing more fun in the whole world than seeing a child open a present at Christmas,' Barbara said. 'To have a six-year-old boy stroke a bicycle with his eyes, not daring to touch and turn to ask, "Is it mine? Really mine?" That's part of my future. The rest is work and I hope some wisdom.'

It was a heart-warming article that might have persuaded some moviegoers to see *Stella Dallas*, but it did not describe Dion's 'Mommy'. When he cried, it was his nanny who came running to take care of him. He was six years old when Stanwyck sent him off to military school, less than ten miles from her ranch. He was not invited home for weekends and holidays nor did she visit him. During the summer he was sent to a camp on Catalina Island. She managed to see him a total of 10 days out of the year in the beginning, but gradually Stanwyck was shutting Dion out of her life and in time reporters stopped asking about him. He disappeared from everything written about Stanwyck as if he never existed. She was now able to begin a new life without the name Fay reminding her of the ugly past.

Helen Ferguson would not admit that Barbara had 'gotten rid of Dion' because she wanted an unencumbered life with Robert Taylor, but Ferguson did not deny it, either: 'This was the happiest time for Barbara, and she devoted herself to making films and loving Robert Taylor – the only two things she ever wanted. I don't think it would have been fair to Dion if she took on the responsibility of bringing him up at home. And, I suppose, she craved the freedom to be with Bob in her spare time. But Barbara had good intentions at first because she wanted Dion to have a good education and the discipline lacking without a father. But I got the impression she regretted adopting a child.'

Frank Fay faded from the limelight except for an occasional nightclub appearance. Then he suddenly burst from oblivion in 1944 as Elwood P. Dowd and his invisible six-foot rabbit *Harvey*, the hit Broadway play. As for his sensational comeback Fay explained, 'How could I help not getting along with a rabbit when I was named after St Francis of Assisi, who was the brother of all the birds and the beasts.' Many critics said Fay was born to play Dowd. *Time* raved, 'Elwood, who on stage could easily become incredible or dismaying, is played to perfection. Fay's manner is almost prim, his delivery slow, his material largely pointless. For one drawled gag like "Had a date with a newspaperwoman the other night – yes, she keeps a stand", there are a dozen droll nothings that are triumphs of timing and intonation.'

Frank Fay died in 1961 at the age of 63 leaving an estimated $200,000 to charity. Dion contested the will and won, but most of the estate went to cover 'debts, liens and other obligations'.

Fay's obituary hinted that the 1937 classic film *A Star is Born* about a famous actor, who commits suicide when his career ends as his wife's star rises, was loosely based on his marriage to Stanwyck. However, William Wellman, director and co-writer of *A Star is Born* said he based the idea on the life of the tragic silent screen actor John Bowers who rowed out into the Pacific Ocean and drowned himself at the age of 49.

On 10 March 1938, Barbara and Bob attended the Academy Award ceremonies at the Biltmore Hotel. The event had been scheduled for 3 March but due to heavy rains and floods, it was postponed for a week. This might have unnerved most actresses, but Barbara was confident about winning Best Actress for *Stella Dallas*. This was her night and she conducted herself as such. Who would have thought that scrawny Ruby Stevens from Brooklyn, the kid with the dirty mouth and face would be sitting with Hollywood's finest waiting for an Oscar so richly deserved?

Stanwyck had some tough competition – Luise Rainer for *The Good Earth*, Greta Garbo in *Camille*, Janet Gaynor for *A Star is Born*, and Irene Dunne in *The Awful Truth*. The favourites were Robert Taylor's co-star in *Camille* and his fiancée Barbara Stanwyck for *Stella Dallas*.

But it was Luise Rainer who was awarded the Oscar for her rich portrayal of the poor and abused Chinese wife, O-Lan. She had won the previous year for *The Great Ziegfeld* and didn't bother to show up. That made it more disappointing for a stunned Barbara. 'My life's blood was in that picture,' she said. 'I should have won.' She never got over it although she was nominated and lost three more times.

CHAPTER EIGHT

Shotgun Wedding

The Mad Miss Manton at RKO was the first of three films Barbara would do with Henry Fonda, the leading man who complemented her most on the screen. Their initial meeting, however, was strained. She was playing a madcap heiress trying to solve a murder with the help of her debutante girlfriends. Fonda hated his role as a newspaper editor and pouted throughout the production. He ignored everyone, including Barbara, except when the cameras were rolling.

'My close relationship with Barbara got off to a rocky start,' Fonda said. 'Three years later in *The Lady Eve* I was delighted to see her, but when I tried to be friendly, she called me a son-of-a-bitch because I had been rude to her in *The Mad Miss Manton*. After she blew her stack we got along famously.'

Barbara was not one to be snubbed. On her list of pet peeves was any actor who brought his or her personal grievances to the set. Fonda's treatment of her was so obvious and deliberate that it was not beneath Stanwyck to give him a dose of his own medicine, but she was attracted to him and he to her. 'Everyone who is close to me knows I've been in love with Barbara Stanwyck since I met her,' Fonda admitted. 'She's a delicious woman. We've never had an affair. She's never encouraged me.'

When Barbara found out what he said about her, she teased, 'He was single when I was single and where was he?'

Joan Crawford did her best to seduce Fonda during *Daisy Kenyon*. She gifted him with a sequin-studded 'cock warmer' on the movie set and asked him to model it for her. Fonda was visibly shaken. 'I've never felt like a terrific lover on screen or off,' he confessed. 'Do you have any idea what it was like out here in Hollywood? Christ! You'd go to dinner at Chasen's. There'd be Tyrone Power at one table with a knockout of a girl, and Bob Taylor with Barbara Stanwyck. Those guys give me a complex. They *looked* like lovers!'

Cecil B. De Mille offered Barbara the lead in his classic film *Union Pacific* with Preston Foster and Joel McCrea for Paramount Pictures. Stanwyck was an excellent choice for the Irish Mollie Monahan, the daughter of the Union Pacific's first engineer, because she grew up with an Irish brogue.

The premiere was almost as exciting and spectacular as the movie itself. De Mille and the cast took a five-day trip on a special train from Los Angeles to Omaha, Nebraska. Celebrations were held in towns and cities along the way and in Omaha the Sioux Indians paraded down the main street. Three theatres premiered *Union Pacific* at the same time. De Mille was a master showman whose films *The Greatest Show on Earth* (1952), *War of the Worlds* (1953) and *The Ten Commandments* (1958) to name a few, are highly regarded to this day. In his autobiography he said he had never worked with an actress 'more cooperative, less temperamental, and a better workman – to use my term of highest compliment – than Barbara Stanwyck.

I have directed and enjoyed working with many fine actresses, some of whom are also good workmen, but when I count over those of whom my memories are unmarred by any unpleasant recollection of friction on the set or unwillingness to do whatever the role required or squalls of temperament or temper, Barbara's name is the first that comes to mind, as one on whom a director can always count to do her work with all her heart.'

The bands played and the Indians marched and DeMille's *Union Pacific* was acclaimed for the action and sound effects, but everyone in Hollywood was talking about Margaret Mitchell's *Gone With the Wind* and who would play Scarlett O'Hara. Barbara wanted to very much but was rejected almost immediately. Producer David Selznick took one look at British actress Vivien Leigh and found his Scarlett. Stanwyck was also turned down for the part of the doomed heiress in *Dark Victory*, and again her rival Bette Davis was the chosen one.

Helen Ferguson commented, 'Barbara was not a femme fatale, but she honestly believed she could play one. I think this was due to the fact that Bob was so crazy about her that it changed her own opinion of herself.'

Stanwyck was perfect for the part of Lorna Moon, an 'orphaned dame from Newark' in Clifford Odets' *Golden Boy*, a hit Broadway play with John Garfield and Frances Farmer about a violinist turned boxer. Columbia Pictures decided to 'search' for an actor to portray Joe Bonaparte in much the same way that Selznick did to find his perfect Scarlett. Director Rouben Mamoulian suggested 21-year-old, newly signed Paramount player, William Holden to the hard-bitten mogul Harry Cohn who stood his ground with Stanwyck a few years before. Holden had the sensitive looks of a violinist and the physique of a boxer, but had no film experience other than bit parts in two movies.

'Can you act?' Cohn asked

'I'm not sure,' Holden said.

'Can you box?'

'No.'

'Can you play the violin?'

'No.'

'Then why the hell are you here?' Cohn grunted.

'Because you sent for me,' Holden responded.

Cohn liked that. He also liked the fact that splitting Holden's salary with Paramount came to just 25 dollars a week.

Filming started on 1 April 1 1939, but problems began within a week when a very nervous and bewildered Holden failed to show up. When he did, he forgot his lines and stumbled over himself. Barbara stepped in when she realised Cohn was going to find another leading man. 'You haven't given him a chance,' she argued. 'Bill's everything you want, but you won't let him alone. I'll work with him if you'll let him stay.' Cohn agreed to give Holden another chance.

Stanwyck stayed on the set every night going over their lines together and showing Bill subtle camera tricks. When they were filming, she encouraged him if they had to do retakes and somehow managed to prevent tempers from flaring. But Mamoulian was a difficult director. He worked each scene the same way: the first was a run-through, the second for tightening, and the third for actual filming. To squeeze all he could from the cast, he did not always roll the camera on the third try. This put everyone on edge, with Holden feeling most of the pressure. He took a few drinks to calm down and began his lifelong battle with the bottle that eventually killed him.

The day Mamoulian played his 'third-take game' with Stanwyck, she swung around and told him off: 'You ask me as a professional to work with you? Then don't ever tell me the camera's rolling when it isn't!'

Barbara not only fought for Holden, she seduced him at some point. He sent dozens of roses to her every year on the starting date of *Golden Boy* to show his appreciation for saving his career. They remained close until his death in 1981.

Fan magazines such as *Photoplay* and *Modern Screen* were very popular with moviegoers in the thirties and forties. They were the link between the great movie stars and their fans. Interviews, however, were carefully edited and all photos touched up and released only by permission of the studios. Compared to the tabloids of today, 'movie magazines' were tame and glamorous, gossipy and innocent. The 'inside stories' were written by press agents or studio publicity people.

But in January 1939, *Photoplay* magazine published a scandalous article, 'Hollywood's Unmarried Husbands and Wives'. It cited five couples, including Carole Lombard and Clark Gable as well as Barbara Stanwyck and Robert Taylor: 'Their houses are on adjoining knolls. The occupants ride together and work together and play together on their time off. If they're asked to a party – they're always invited together like man and wife. Or they spend a quiet evening together at either one or the other's place.'

The article relates the tragic story of actress Jean Harlow who was reportedly planning to marry William Powell when she died suddenly in 1937. *Photoplay* used this example to admonish the naughty affairs: 'And that, it seems, would point a lesson to the unique coterie of Hollywood's unwed couples. Bob Taylor and Barbara Stanwyck could get married if they wanted to . . . Carole Lombard and Clark Gable and the other steady company couples might swing it if they tried a little harder.

'For nobody, not even Hollywood's miracle men, has ever improved on the good old-fashioned, satisfying institution of holy matrimony. And, until something better comes along, the best way to hunt happiness when you're in love is with a preacher, a marriage license and a bagful of rice.'

MGM mogul Louis B. Mayer threatened to sue *Photoplay* and ban them from communicating with any of his contract players. In February the magazine issued a retraction and public apology, but the damage had been done. Bob and Barbara announced their formal engagement, and put both ranches up for sale.

Mayer was more concerned about Clark Gable's getting a divorce. Above all, MGM wanted no blemish of scandal to crop up around the stars in *Gone With the Wind* that was scheduled to premiere in Atlanta on 15 December 1939 and in New York on 19 December. Vivien Leigh was not allowed to be photographed with her lover Laurence Olivier because they were both in the process of divorcing their spouses. Paulette Goddard had been considered for the part of Scarlett O'Hara but was eliminated because she could not prove her marriage to Charlie Chaplin. She claimed that the Mayor of Catalina performed the ceremony, but Catalina had no mayor. Goddard and Chaplin were also mentioned in the *Photoplay* article.

MGM used its influence to negotiate Gable's divorce and loan him the money his wife demanded before she agreed to go to Reno to dissolve the marriage. He married Carole Lombard on 29 March 1939 during filming of *Gone With the Wind*. Louis B. Mayer waited until the publicity of one famous wedding died down before planning another one.

The cameras were rolling on Robert Taylor and Hedy Lamarr in *Lady of the Tropics* when Mayer stopped production for 24 hours. MGM made arrangements for a wedding, and on 13 May Barbara and Bob drove to San Diego. Joining them at the home of Mr and Mrs Thomas Whelan were Zeppo and Marion Marx; Ida Koverman, Mayer's secretary; Buck Mack, Barbara's godfather; and Dale Franz, a friend. The wedding party had a buffet supper, and after midnight, to avoid being married on the unlucky thirteenth day, the ceremony began in a room filled with roses.

Barbara wore a blue silk dress with a hat borrowed from her hairdresser, Holly Barnes, whose marriage Stanwyck had witnessed the day before. Buck Mack gave the bride away.

She was very calm and spoke her marriage vows distinctly. Taylor, in a brown business suit, and having been rushed into the marriage by MGM, was visibly shaken and mumbled his vows.

The bride's wedding ring, a slender gold band, circled with rubies, matched the bracelet Bob had given her.

At two in the afternoon the Taylors met the press at a reception at the Victor Hugo Café in Beverly Hills. Joel McCrea was the first to telephone congratulations, and William Holden sent a telegram – 'Gosh, what a blow!' and signed it Golden Boy. The newlyweds said they had taken out their marriage licence three days earlier under their real names, Ruby Stevens, age 31, and Spangler Arlington Brugh, age 27. At the time they did not know when they would be married.

Taylor confessed years later that MGM masterminded the whole affair. 'I wasn't sure if I was in love,' he said. 'The only thing I was allowed to do was say "I do". When I went to England, it was my first time away from everyone close to me and my career was on the line. I think I wanted Barbara to come to England to marry me just to relieve my panic and loneliness. I liked Barbara. She had done a lot of favours for me. There was no one else I admired more and no one else I cared to be with, but I kinda got over the urge to marry. When I knew it had to happen, I didn't know if I was in love. I wasn't sure at all.'

The Daily News wrote, 'The Number One Heart Throb of

the movies eloped with Barbara Stanwyck leaving the set of *Lady of the Tropics* and the beautiful Hedy Lamarr. There, there, girls, bear up and try not to take it so hard. You know it was ordained by fate.'

The unwritten consensus of the press and friends of the newlyweds was that Barbara Stanwyck married Robert Taylor, not the other way around.

After the reception, Barbara returned to her ranch, and the groom went to see his hysterical mother, Ruth, who had called the doctor for a sedative. When Bob walked through the door, she covered her face with her hands and wept. They had a long talk, but the word 'wedding' was not mentioned. She referred to the marriage as 'it'.

Bob knew his mother would be depressed and ill. He assured her nothing would change and tried to joke about it. 'Oh, mother, you know when I'm working here in town sometimes I get so tired I don't feel like driving out to the ranch, so I'll stay here with you.'

They had coffee, but Ruth complained that she felt sick and weak. 'Will you check my heartbeat every so often during the night, son, just to make sure I'm all right?'

So Robert Taylor spent his wedding night with his mother.

The following morning he was back on the set with Hedy Lamarr, and Barbara finished *Golden Boy*.

MGM considered co-starring the newlyweds in another picture, but this never happened. The Taylors took a brief honeymoon at the 72-acre estate of playwright Moss Hart in Bucks County, Pennsylvania, a popular getaway for the Broadway crowd in the thirties. Hart's impressive stone farmhouse had a library, swimming pool and acres of pine trees overlooking the Delaware River. Bob considered buying property nearby and Barbara said she'd think it over which meant no. The country was fine with her for a week or so but she bored easily without the hustle and bustle of city life.

Stanwyck's co-starred with Fred MacMurray in one of her better films *Remember the Night* released in January 1940. The title had little to do with the story of a shoplifter (Barbara) befriended by an assistant District Attorney (MacMurray) who cannot find it in his heart to prosecute her on Christmas Eve and takes her home to spend the holidays with his mother. They fall in love, but she goes to jail, and he promises to wait for her. As usual, Barbara is at her best playing the reformed bad girl. Written by the talented and eccentric Preston Sturges, *Remember the Night* was applauded by critics who urged moviegoers to make a point of seeing it. *The New York Times* wrote, 'After dallying too long with the leftovers of 1939, the screen has awakened finally to new year and new entertainment responsibilities. *Remember the Night* is a real curtain raiser for 1940, the first work of reassurance Hollywood has offered since '39 went into the past. It is a memorable film.'

A remarkable trait of Barbara's was revealed during production of *Remember the Night*. After she had been dismissed for the day, it was discovered that she was required for another scene. Frantically the assistant director ran to her dressing room and found, to his amazement, that she was still in costume. 'I never leave until everyone else does,' she said, 'just in case.'

Robert Taylor's role as a navy ensign in *Fight Command* (1940) was in reality the beginning of the end of his marriage. He became so involved with aeroplanes that he decided to take flying lessons. If Bob wasn't in the air he spent his spare time fishing with Spencer Tracy or at the Hunt Club with Clark Gable. Barbara was terrified of flying and afraid of guns. When Bob polished his rifles in the living room she often read him the riot act. 'Every time you aim that thing you scare me to death,' she exclaimed. But his passion for flying upset her more. 'Bob's not satisfied on the ground these days,' she complained, but no matter how much he pleaded with her to fly with him, she cringed at the very thought. Her reasoning was, 'We don't spend enough time together.' That was her excuse to get him down from the sky despite her putting in longer hours at work than he did.

Their ranches had not been sold, but Barbara was fed up with commuting and began looking for a furnished house to lease in town. She found one in Bel Air, a fashionable part of Los Angeles at 423 North Faring Road, that was owned by actress Coleen Moore's mother, and signed a one-year lease. Bob was stunned and very upset and tried to talk her out of it.

'I don't want to live in a furnished house,' he exclaimed.

'It's only temporary.'

'What about the horses?'

'I sold my stable to Zeppo and I'm sure he'll buy yours.'

'What's the big rush?'

'We're both so damn busy. Our days off conflict, and when they coincide, we're not together.'

'But my gun rack . . .'

She shrugged.

'And my kitchen is designed to my liking. What about my utensils?'

'I call them gadgets,' she laughed. 'Hell, all we really need is a can opener.'

'I won't be comfortable living in someone else's house,' he said.

'Just keep reminding yourself it's only temporary, Junior.'

This was their first major argument aside from his passion for planes and it led to more flying hours for Taylor. 'I am alive up there,' he told a friend. 'Nobody's telling me what to do and how to do it. No telephones and no traffic. Free as hell.'

Barbara had no spare time. Completely dedicated to her career, she was either busy reading scripts or studying her lines or filming. She was her own boss whereas Taylor was assigned to pictures, told who his co-stars would be and when to report for work. He was always on time and knew his lines, but the preparation and productions were entirely different to Barbara's, who was responsible for herself and no one else. When Bob left the movie set for the day, he left the character he was playing behind. Barbara brought hers home.

They were both uninterested in socialising and entertaining, but Bob was expected to go out two or three times a week for publicity purposes. 'MGM demanded it,' Barbara said. When they stayed home, Bob prepared the meals. 'Bob loves the kitchen,' she said in an interview. 'He collects cookbooks, and all kinds of gadgets. I can't boil water. When he's in the house, Bob spends his time in the kitchen where he's the happiest. Otherwise, he's looking out the window. I always had a book to read, but he couldn't sit still long enough for that. Or he fell asleep and he could do that in a second.' Barbara was an insomniac.

Taylor was doing insignificant films – *The Crowd Roars*, *Stand Up and Fight*, and *Lucky Night*, all in keeping with his new macho image. 'When I was just about convinced I had been forgotten,' he said, 'MGM gave me *Waterloo Bridge* in 1940. This was an actor's dream come true and the role fitted me like a pair of custom-made shoes.' It remained Taylor's favourite during his long career.

Since it was the custom of all English officers during World War I to wear a moustache, he was required to grow one – the moustache he would shave off and grow again with monotonous regularity throughout his lifetime. It did, however, give him the distinction and maturity that transformed a juvenile pretty face into one of character.

It was Stanwyck's good fortune to co-star again with Henry Fonda in a comedy written and directed by one of Barbara's greatest admirers, Preston Sturges, who had promised he would come up with a comedy for her. 'He kept his word – and how,' she said. 'By that time I wasn't under contract to Paramount and he'd have to borrow me. Which would kill it, I figured. He also wanted to borrow Hank Fonda from Fox – another piece of intriguing casting. Hank had been Zanuck's Abraham Lincoln in so many things, whether his name was Tom Joad or Jesse James. How did Sturges know he was a sensational light comedian? Somehow *The Lady Eve* all came together.'

Fonda plays an eccentric millionaire who ditches Stanwyck after he finds out she's a card sharp. To get even with him, she poses as the very British Lady Eve. Her plan is to marry Fonda and let him down with a thud on their honeymoon. She succeeds, but still loves him and reverts back to her old self and the woman he really wants, after all.

Barbara literally trips Henry up five times in the film. If her foot isn't in his path, he manages to fall down by himself. Because of these amusing mishaps, usually in a white dinner jacket, Fonda might have walked away with *The Lady Eve*, but Barbara's reaction to his blunders makes the film a sheer delight.

As Eve Harrington, she's a con woman who fleeces rich men in card games and whatever else comes along. She plays with Fonda's Hopsie, who is almost paralysed by her toying with his hair and earlobes, flirting and teasing him into marriage. On their disastrous honeymoon, she tells him on their wedding bed outlandish and false tales of many other husbands. Wearing only pyjamas, Hopsie jumps off the train into a mud puddle.

While Fonda spills gravy or cocktails all over himself, Stanwyck looks lovely in an elegant wardrobe designed by Edith Head who recalled, 'Barbara hated high fashion. She cared less what she was wearing as long as it wasn't form-fitting. The gowns created for Eve were tight and slick. I knew Barbara could wear them very well because she had fine posture and a slim figure. The first dress she put on was a clinging black crepe with a very high and very tight cummerbund.

'She was suffering at first. Barbara kept her back to the mirror and would not turn around. She said that people notice you sideways or from the back, but I insisted she face the mirror. When she did, Barbara was delighted, but too modest to admit it. From then on she wanted to wear high fashion.

'We had only one dispute and she won. Most actresses model their costumes for the director in front of the camera with hands on the hips and a flare, turning around once or twice. Barbara walked towards the camera, stood still and then walked away. I told her to pose. She glared at me and said she was not a model and had no intention of acting like one. That was that.

'*The Lady Eve* changed both our lives. It was Barbara's first high-fashion picture and her biggest transition in costuming. She was quite trim and had a better shape than most of the other actresses around. She possessed what some designers considered to be a figure "problem" – a long waist and comparatively low rear end . . . I took advantage of her long waist to create the illusion that her derriere was just as perfectly placed as any other star's.'

Stanwyck praised Head for changing her image. 'Edith always covered her mouth when she talked and I didn't know why. Finally she showed me her teeth and they were awful. Some were missing. She said dentists had told her nothing could be done so I sent her to my dentist because he had fixed me up.'

Edith Head was bisexual, leaning towards the Sapphic side. There were rumours, of course, about her and Barbara over the years. More importantly, Stanwyck was allowed to keep the glamorous gowns she wore in *The Lady Eve* that was chosen by the National Board of Review as one of the best pictures released in 1941.

CHAPTER NINE

Lana

While Taylor was making *Waterloo Bridge* in England, Barbara received a phone call from her former lover and favourite director, Frank Capra, who had formed his own production company. 'How would you like to make *Meet John Doe* with Gary Cooper?' he asked.

'Honey, send the script right over!'

'I don't have one yet.'

'Is my part an honest one?'

'Yes, it is.'

'Then I'll do it!'

Gary Cooper and Walter Brennan also agreed to do the picture without reading the script. 'There is no one like Frank Capra,' Barbara said with great feeling. 'He's in a class all by himself. It's a joy to watch him work. You make other pictures to live, but you live to make a Capra picture.' The romance with him long over, she was attracted to the well-endowed Gary Cooper as most women were, but Stanwyck remained faithful to Bob. In *Meet John Doe*, Barbara plays a cynical reporter who invents 'John Doe', a disillusioned drifter, and his threatened suicide jump from the Empire State Building on Christmas Eve.

Because the story deals with the threat of fascism, Capra filmed four different endings, all of which were screened in selected theatres. Capra allowed the audiences to decide which they preferred before doing the fifth and final version. John Doe is convinced by Barbara and other drifters not to take his own life, a classy ending to a classy film.

The New York Times strongly suggested that everyone make the acquaintance of John Doe. *Film Daily* picked *Meet John Doe* as one of the top ten best pictures of the year. The *New York World Telegram* said Stanwyck and Cooper were in top form. 'They don't come any better than this one,' they wrote about the film.

Movies were better than ever just prior to World War II. Good scripts were abundant and the great stars of the Golden Era made them come to life. Though Taylor wasn't Oscar material, he was given a pat on the back by critics for *Escape* with Norma Shearer, *Billy the Kid*, and *When Ladies Meet* with Greer Garson and Joan Crawford.

Stanwyck was riding the crest as an actress, but losing a grip on the man she loved. Taylor took the title role in *Johnny Eager*, a gangster who destroys himself for the love of a girl. Actor Van Heflin, who plays Johnny's drunken confidant, won an Oscar for Best Supporting Actor in 1942. This film had special meaning for Bob because he fell helplessly in love with his 21-year-old leading lady, Lana Turner. Nicknamed the Sweater Girl, she was suing Artie Shaw for divorce after less than a year of marriage.

Taylor told his best friend, Tom Purvis that he and Lana were 'bursting' with passion during production, but did nothing about it until they finished filming – at least, that was what he claimed. 'I had to have her if only for one night.'

It was more than that, however. Barbara appeared at MGM one day to confront the lovers, and Louis B. Mayer barred Stanwyck from the set.

Bob said in an interview that his newest co-star, Lana Turner, was perfectly proportioned and not as 'busty' as her pin-up photos suggest. 'Her face is delicate and beautiful,' he said. 'I have never seen lips like hers and though I was never known to run after blondes, Lana could be the exception. I couldn't take my eyes off her. She had the voice of a breathless little girl. I don't think she knew how to speak without being sexy. When she said, "Good morning," I melted. She is the type of girl a guy would risk five years in jail for rape.'

Lana wrote in her memoirs, 'Bob had the kind of looks I could fall for, and we were attracted to each other from the beginning. I'll admit I flirted with him – but for me it was nothing more than that, since he was married to Barbara Stanwyck. Certainly our mutual attraction didn't harm our love scenes.' Lana went on to say she felt a pang of fear when Bob said he wasn't happy at home and that he was in love with her.

Lana was a product of the MGM studio system and had been taught how to deal with situations like this. Admit only to romance, never to sex. Columnist Sheila Graham said it was interesting to read the autobiographies of former movie queens who remember only a few of the men in their lives. 'Let them do whatever they want,' Graham mused, 'but they should tell the truth. In their books, all these girls were trembling and terrified and shy with men. To hear Lana tell it you'd think she did "it" only once. She had to admit to that because she had a daughter.'

Lana's daughter Cheryl wrote in her recent book *Lana: the Memories, the Myths, the Movies* that her mother's affair with Bob was intense, but his asking Stanwyck for a divorce frightened her.

Robert Taylor had his share of women, but was not one to

brag about his conquests whether he was married or single. His close buddy Tom Purvis admits that Bob told him about his brief affair with Lana many years later, but doubts that he would have asked Stanwyck for a divorce unless there was more to the relationship than just a flirtation.

MGM publicity chief Howard Strickling said, 'Taylor was my favourite because we could reason with him, and he was a small town boy at heart. Our stars were always falling in love with each other but when the picture was finished so was the affair. Lana was a first for Taylor and he fell very hard. Later on he took this kind of thing in stride.'

No one was better at that than Clark Gable, who co-starred with Lana in *Honky Tonk*. After only a few days of working together, rumours of a romance were so rampant that Gable's wife, Carole Lombard, threatened to confront the 'lovers' on the movie set and 'kick them both in the ass!' Her fights with Clark over Lana were explosive. 'I'll have her fired!' she threatened.

'You can't do that!' Gable argued.

'Then I'll have you fired!'

MGM boss Louis B. Mayer alerted guards not to allow Mrs Clark Gable beyond the front gate without notifying her husband and she was eventually barred from the set of *Honky Tonk*.

Choreographer Jack Cole said, 'I've worked with them all – Rita Hayworth, Betty Grable, Lana Turner . . . the whole bloody bit, and what's very curious, well, Lana Turner's a little different because she really liked men, she liked to fuck a lot. But most of the others, it's the idea of it.'

MGM finished *Honky Tonk* in record time to separate Turner and Gable. She was rushed into the arms of 'Johnny Eager'. When producer Norman Lear was asked to name the sexiest woman in the world he replied, 'Lana Turner, as she was

Barbara with her first husband, Frank Fay, in 1930.

Stanwyck was devastated when she did not win the Oscar for best actress in Stella Dallas (1937).

Barbara and Robert Taylor meet the press after their elopement on May 14, 1939.

Henry Fonda with Stanwyck on the set of the Lady Eve (1941).

Fred MacMurray and Barbara plot a murder in Double Indemnity (1944).

Stanwyck's role of a fear-crazed invalid in Sorry Wrong Number (1955) was so exhausting, her hair turned white.

Barbara and Elvis Presley barely tolerated each other filming Roustabout in 1964.

Kirk Douglas presents Stanwyck with the Golden Globe award in 1986.

held in the arms of Robert Taylor in the terrace scene in *Johnny Eager.*'

Barbara was devastated when Bob asked her for a divorce. She hid out in the home of her maid Harriet Corey for a few days until the press found out where she was. She returned home, but on 7 October 1941 Stanwyck was rushed to Cedars of Lebanon Hospital with severed arteries on her wrist and arm. Attempted suicide? No, Bob told reporters. She was struggling to open a jammed window. Using the heel of her hand, she had broken the glass. Barbara never tried to explain the cuts on her arm. And she never forgave 'the other woman'. Forty years later Lana learned that Stanwyck was staying at the same hotel and called her to have a drink. Barbara hung up the telephone.

When gangster Johnny Eager was shot down and killed at the end of the movie, Stanwyck could stop worrying because Lana then began filming *Somewhere I'll Find You* opposite Clark Gable – again. Carole Lombard was so upset, she flew home from an Indiana bond rally instead of taking the train as planned. She was killed instantly when her plane crashed near Las Vegas on 16 January 1942. Lana wrote in her memoirs, 'I heard a dreadful rumour about her uneasiness over my working with Clark.'

Gable and Lombard had been married less than two years and were an ideal couple despite his harmless philandering. Stanwyck and Taylor were not an ideal couple. Hollywood insiders knew they had marital problems from the onset and reporters were waiting for another 'broken window' episode to pounce. Barbara met with the press to dispel rumours. 'Bob is tired,' she explained. 'He has made several pictures in a row with no time off and he's resting now. He wanted to take some extensive flying lessons and took his instructor to the Odlum Ranch in Palm Springs. We are by no means separated and there are people, I suppose, who are jealous and would like to see me take a fall. Since my career has been so successful lately, they attacked my marriage.' Ironically, Barbara had said the same thing to reporters when she and Frank Fay were having marital problems. 'Bob and I are building a house in Beverly Hills. Does that sound as if we are getting a divorce?'

Six months earlier Howard Strickling helped Bob compose a letter, dated 14 March 1941, to Jim Reid of *Motion Picture Magazine:*

> Dear Jim,
> Thank you for the opportunity of replying to the rumour which seems to have been circulating around recently. Unfortunately, it is an opportunity which is too seldom granted people in this business.
>
> Barbara and I were married two years ago for reasons which are common. I believe, to any two people who decide to take that step, namely love, mutual interests and a pretty good understanding of each other. So far as we are concerned these elements still exist.
>
> The rumour, though unfortunate, did not come as a surprise to either Barbara or myself. Actually, we have been expecting it. It seems almost inevitable that when picture people have been married over a year, rumours of this sort arise. May I assure you and hope that you will assure your readers in turn, that all such rumours are entirely unfounded and untrue. Thanks again from Barbara and myself.
> Sincerely,
> Bob

Maybe moviegoers were satisfied with the Taylors insisting all was rosy on the home front but close friends saw a strained marriage even before the Lana Turner incident. Barbara continued her maternal ways referring to Bob as Junior and he called her the Queen. They were apart so often maybe they forgot each other's names. Paradoxically, though, it was those career separations that held the marriage together as long as it did. On the very few trips Barbara and Bob made together, he would fly and she would find other means of transportation to meet him at their destination.

Bob, who in his early film career had enjoyed going back to his hometown in Nebraska, stayed away after his marriage. He didn't think Barbara would fit in and she had no intention of trying to impress his old friends. Taylor's classic understatement to reporters, 'Miss Stanwyck is not the sort of woman I would have met in Nebraska,' always got chuckles in the pressroom. Then there was his mother Ruth, a domineering influence in his life. Inevitably there was no love between her and Barbara – both wanting to be the boss. He had two mothers; one he would visit once a week and the other shared his bed.

Though Barbara complained about his hunting, she bought him several expensive rifles to show how sorry she was for complaining about his hobbies. When Bob got a motorcycle, Barbara worried sick every time he rode it. Yet she bought him a newer and more expensive one, hoping he would forgive her nagging. She showed him how to ride it, too, while photographers clicked away in disbelief.

Helen Ferguson said, 'It's true Barbara treated Bob like a little boy. She was too protective. He wanted to be the man of the house, and Barbara didn't know how to accept this even though she said he was the boss. I remember how much he loved dogs, but Barbara was allergic to them. One day Bob found her sitting on top of a stepladder reading a script in the living room. "Get yourself a mutt," she said. "It won't bother me up here." Barbara gave him a hard time about such things and Bob soon forgot about it. Then she'd give in and he wasn't interested any more.'

Barbara's exceptionally deep love for Taylor was an emotion she could not control. She had the capability to handle any problem that confronted her professionally, and the confidence to see it through, but she could not govern love and fidelity. Bob's confessed love for Lana Turner and asking her for a divorce nearly killed her.

CHAPTER TEN

The War Years

When the Japanese bombed Pearl Harbor on 7 December 1941, Hollywood was suddenly just another town of Americans who were anxious to volunteer for the war effort. President Roosevelt, however, stressed the importance of entertainment for public morale, but the majority of eligible male stars tried to enlist. L.B. Mayer told his family of stars, 'Clark Gable's drawing only $66 a month in the Air Corp. The least we can do is take a cut in salary.' Sam Goldwyn told his players, 'Don't think of the money, think of your country.'

Bette Davis founded the Hollywood Canteen where servicemen mingled with the movie stars who cooked, washed dishes, entertained and danced with young men in uniform. Gary Cooper went to Washington in an effort to publicise the importance of motion pictures during wartime. 'This is not the time to cut down production in Hollywood,' he said. 'The more taxes an actor can pay, the more he is helping to win the war.' The Defense Department was also well aware of how important movies were to public morale. Every week 80 million people went to movie theatres that were open around the clock. Frank Capra was given the rank of major to organise the Army Pictorial Service, which would make thousands of training films ranging from the subject of venereal diseases to assembling M-1 rifles.

Jimmy Stewart joined the air force and became a bomber pilot. He saw a good deal of action and retired as a brigadier general. Clark Gable joined the air force at the age of 41, went through basic training and volunteered for dangerous missions over Germany. Shattered over the death of Carole Lombard, Gable had a death wish and did not expect to come home. Tyrone Power joined the marines and saw action in the South Pacific. Henry Fonda spent three years in the navy and was awarded the bronze star for bravery in combat.

Robert Taylor was eager to get into uniform and see action. Barbara 'forbade' him to enlist but he did so behind her back. At 31 he volunteered for combat many times but was more valuable as a naval aviation instructor.

Louis B. Mayer was very upset that his leading men were 'going to war' and used his influence to keep them out of harm's way. Taylor's last film before going into the Navy was the controversial *Song of Russia*. He did not want to do the movie for political reasons, claiming it was pro-Soviet. Bob had many meetings with Mayer, explaining he could not find it in his heart to do the picture. 'It's just a boy-girl love story set to Tchaikovsky's music,' Mayer said.

'As far as I'm concerned, it's "Commie" from beginning to end,' Taylor complained bitterly.

Mayer sent for an aide to the late President Roosevelt who was the head of the Office of War Information's film division to discuss it with Taylor. He said the United States Government was interested in having the movie made and wanted other producers to film similar themes in order to influence the

American people in favour of Russia. Taylor emphasised that he was waiting for his orders to report for Navy duty and was more interested in getting into uniform than 'trying to promote some "pink" propaganda shit for loyal Americans to watch.' The head of OWI, however, managed to convince Bob that he should reconsider, and reluctantly he gave in. Taylor played a musical conductor touring the Soviet Union who falls in love with a Russian girl (Susan Peters.)

Bob hated every minute of it.

A week before Taylor was sworn into the Navy as Spangler Arlington Brugh, he and Barbara became founding members of the Motion Picture Alliance for the Preservation of American Ideals. The Alliance was both a backlash against the guild that in the last ten years had unionised the industry and reaction against the robust left wing of intellectuals and artists of the New Deal. The Alliance members included people Barbara and Bob had worked with – directors King Vidor, Clarence Brown and Sam Wood, actors Gary Cooper, Clark Gable, Ward Bond and John Wayne. Joining this group were author Ayn Rand, columnist Hedda Hopper and actresses Ginger Rogers and Irene Dunne. Walt Disney and other Hollywood celebrities would join eventually. Newspaper magnate William Randolph Hearst was an important and loyal supporter.

Though Barbara and Bob had little in common, they were both staunch Republicans, though she was not as outspoken as he was. He would go public in this matter while Barbara preferred to be a quiet participant. She felt obligated to nobody and resented a new sneaky society who hid behind scripts to preach leftist dictates. She donated generously to the Alliance and held meetings in her house when Bob was taking basic training in February 1943. He applied once again for active duty and was turned down. Instead he was assigned to the Navy's Aviation Volunteer Transport Division as a Lieutenant (junior grade), the customary rank given to men over thirty who had a civilian pilot's licence. Taylor had 110 flying hours to his credit. He took his basic training at the Naval Air Station in Dallas, Texas, and then transferred to the Naval Instructors' school in New Orleans as a student. He volunteered for active duty again, but was finally convinced he was too valuable as an instructor. He hadn't been flying for almost a year and requested a refresher course. 'But don't send me up with some twenty-one year old who'll run all over the base telling everyone I can't do a slow roll or inverted spin.'

The Chief of Flight said he would assign an older instructor, Tom Purvis, who became Taylor's co-pilot. This was the beginning of a lasting friendship between the two men. 'We got up to about five thousand feet in an open plane,' Purvis recalled, 'and I told him to get ready for a right slow roll. It was perfect but when we came out of it Bob looked like he was going to throw up. I asked him what was wrong.'

'Hell, I just lost my cigarette lighter. It's down there in the Mississippi River!' Apparently Bob had forgotten to button the shin pocket of his summer coverall. He told Purvis the lighter had been a gift from Barbara – a solid gold Zippo bearing a raised replica of the Naval Station emblem and the date (1943). 'She'll flip her lid! What the hell do I tell her?'

'Tell her it's at the bottom of the Mississippi!' Tom laughed. 'I think it's funny.'

'It was careless of me.'

'What's the big deal?'

'You don't know Barbara,' was Bob's reply.

She replaced it, however, on her only visit to New Orleans while Taylor was stationed there. He arranged a party for her at the elegant Roosevelt Hotel, but there was little publicity because Taylor wouldn't allow it. He was all Navy now and cared little about what was happening in Hollywood. On one of his furloughs to California he agreed to pose with Barbara in their home. He looked very young with his butch haircut and Barbara very mature and sophisticated in her dressing gown and upswept hair. She looked more like a mother than a wife. 'He looks so young with that haircut,' she said looking up at him adoringly. 'He's lost ten pounds. He's the most handsome man I've ever seen, but he looks eighteen. People will think I'm his mother.'

While Bob was drawing his lieutenant's pay and loving it, Barbara was the highest salaried woman in the movies – $400,000 in 1943 – out-earning the other cinema queens, Bette Davis, Greer Garson and Betty Grable. But Stanwyck was seldom listed in the popularity polls because, according to Helen Ferguson, she was not a sex symbol. Other than missing her husband she was very content. So was Taylor, who told Tom Purvis, 'I've never been happier since my days in Nebraska.'

'I think Bob could have stayed in the Navy,' Tom said. 'He hated the thought of going back to Hollywood . . . back to the phoniness and back to playing the handsome guy who always got the girl and pretending that his marriage was near perfect when it was far from that. I know that many people in Hollywood thought he was gay, but I saw him in a fury if a man made a pass at him or tried to reach him by phone. And they chased him. That was the only time I saw Bob lose his temper. I don't pretend to know everything about him, but I did know Taylor for the last twenty-five years of his life and he was all man. And he never fooled around on Barbara when he was in the Navy, either. As for his career, he wanted to get into films and was grateful to MGM but he often said he'd like to buy a farm in Nebraska and forget about Hollywood. He meant it, too, but where does Robert Taylor hide? Five thousand feet in the air, I guess. That's why he loved to fly. There was peace nowhere else.'

Barbara found peace on the ground and in front of the camera . . .

You Belong to Me at Columbia was another hilarious picture Barbara made with Henry Fonda whose character made a delightful fool of himself, because he is so jealous of the men patients seen by his doctor wife, played by Barbara. Critics loved the picture. *The New York Times* called it 'a bit of well-turned fun'. This would be her last film with Fonda and she later said she regretted it. He did, too. 'I told my wife and kids I was in love with Barbara Stanwyck,' he said. Writer Herman Mankiewicz was crazy about her, too. 'I could just dream of being married to her, having a little cottage out in the hills, roses around the door. I'd come home from the office, tired and weary, and I'd spy Barbara there through the door, walking in with an apple pie she'd just baked herself. And no drawers.'

Mr Mankiewicz had a delightful sense of humour.

Stanwyck attracted men who liked tough women – dames who talked dirty and gave the impression they wanted wild sex without any commitments. She sat with her feet up on the table and gave men the look of 'I dare you. If you do, I'll kiss you and then throw you out of the room on your ass because you're worthless'.

Barbara did not exude romance. She had an aura of crude clutches and heavy breathing, grass stains on her 'drawers' and cursing when the deed was done. Mankiewicz could sense this. In *Ball of Fire* she 'played herself' as striptease artiste, Sugarpuss O'Shea, who helps a professor – played by Gary Cooper – work on slang for his new dictionary. After Ginger Rogers and Jean Arthur turned down the role, Goldwyn gave the lead to Barbara, who was nominated for her second Oscar. She would lose to Joan Fontaine in *Suspicion.*

Barbara was enthusiastic about doing *The Great Man's Lady* made at Paramount. Portraying the pioneer bride of Joel McCrea, she ages to 107, which was one of her greatest challenges. Stanwyck handled her ageing from a teenage bride to matriarch skilfully, but critics considered the film mediocre. It dragged on with clichés despite the superb direction of William Wellman. 'It broke my heart that it was not a success,' Barbara said.

The Gay Sisters at Warner Brothers was anything but gay. Barbara plays the hard-hearted sister who tricks George Brent into marriage for a legacy. After he forces her to spend their wedding night together, she leaves him. Several years later Brent, gets custody of their son. Barbara's love for the child and for Brent bring them all together in the end.

In contrast, Stanwyck made *Lady of Burlesque* (*Striptease Lady* in the United Kingdon), a United Artists production, based on a novel, *The G-String Murders*, written by the most famous stripper, Gypsy Rose Lee. Among Barbara's song and dance routines with high heels, cartwheels, and splits was her throaty rendition of 'Take it Off the E-String, Play it on the G-String.' *The New York Times* wrote, 'Miss Stanwyck takes to scanty gowns like fish to water and proves in the dance numbers that she hasn't forgotten her early chorus training on Broadway.' Her boyfriend in the film is Michael O'Shea, who complemented Barbara nicely as she bumps and grinds for an enthusiastic audience. But was it a good idea for her to make the film? 'She did it for the fun and diversion,' Joan Crawford said. 'A serious actress needs to break away and cut loose once in a while. Besides, the world was at war. People needed laughter, and our fighting men wanted to see movies like *Lady of Burlesque*. I think it gave Barbara an earthy quality that people didn't think she possessed.'

Though the film was good entertainment, many people

were embarrassed for Barbara who, they felt, cheapened herself in the role of Dixie Daisy. But what the hell did she care what anyone thought? She was married to the illegally handsome Robert Taylor and making more money than other actresses who were doing goody- goody parts in better films.

Hoofer Iris Adrian, who joined the cast of *Lady of Burlesque*, told Barbara that Frank had stopped drinking. 'He was having an affair with actress Bette Keane who became pregnant and gave up her career to have his baby,' she said. Stanwyck wasn't interested, but it had to be a blow to her ego that Fay had the child she couldn't give him.

Flesh and Fantasy with Charles Boyer and Edward G. Robinson was an anthology of three loosely connected cult tales with romantic and ironic twists. The film was released in 1943 with little recognition.

It made little difference to Barbara once she got her hands on Billy Wilder's script for *Double Indemnity*. She could feel the part of Phyllis Dietrichson, but was reluctant to play a cold-blooded killer. 'I wasn't sure I wanted to do anything like this even though I adored the story,' she said. Meanwhile, Wilder talked to Fred MacMurray, who felt the same way Barbara did. He had always played the easygoing nice guy and didn't think the public would accept him as a dirty louse. 'I'm not sure about doing it,' he said. Wilder mentioned casually that Stanwyck had agreed to do it if MacMurray was her leading man. 'Okay. That's good enough for me. I'll do it.'

'Fred didn't know that George Raft had rejected the part,' Wilder said. 'No actor wanted to play a murderer in those days except a guy like Raft, and he turned it down.'

The grim story of Phyllis Dietrichson persuading insurance salesman Walter Neff to fix her husband up with an accident policy and murder him to collect $100,000 on its double indemnity clause, is a classic to this day. Stanwyck wore a blonde wig and sleazy ankle bracelet to emphasise how cheap and seductive Phyllis was. They collect the insurance money but kill each other in the end.

Barbara recalled her apprehension. 'I thought the role was going to finish me. But it was the best script I had ever been offered. It's brilliant but what is amazing is that not one word was changed while we were shooting. Billy had it all there, and I mean *all* – everything you see on the screen was in the script.

'When I mention "atmosphere" in the *Double Indemnity* – that gloomy, horrible house that the Dietrichsons lived in, the slit of sunlight through those heavy drapes – you could smell that death was in the air, you understood why she wanted to get out of there, away, no matter how. And for an actress, let me tell you the way those sets were lit – the house, Walter's apartment, those dark shadows, those slices of harsh light at strange angles – all that helped my performance.'

Released by Paramount in September 1944, *Double Indemnity* was a hit. *Time* magazine said it was the 'season's nattiest, nastiest, most satisfying melodrama'. The picture was nominated for seven Academy Awards, including best picture and best actress, but the film did not win in any category. This was Stanwyck's third Oscar bid, but she lost to Ingrid Bergman for *Gaslight*. 'I'm beginning to feel like one of Bing Crosby's also-ran horses,' Barbara said, trying to make light of her disappointment.

Before going to New York City on a war-bond drive, Barbara made the charming *Christmas in Connecticut* with Dennis Morgan at Warner Brothers. She plays a domesticated food and home columnist for *Smart Housekeeping* magazine, despite the fact she doesn't know how to turn on an oven or vacuum cleaner. When her boss forces her to entertain a young serviceman, Barbara's 'Martha Stewart' has to invent a husband, a baby and a sprawling summer home in Connecticut. The movie focused on a typical New England holiday with romantic sleigh rides, dancing the Virginia Reel and decorating a floor-to-ceiling Christmas tree.

In January 1945, Robert Taylor was in New York City to promote the Navy film, *The Fighting Lady*. Barbara joined him and made it clear to the press that her being in the East was to see her husband and to sell war bonds. When columnist Earl Wilson telephoned her, she consented to an interview, but when he arrived at the Taylors' hotel suite, he found himself alone with Bob who said Barbara would be there shortly. She finally appeared, but rushed into the room, said a fleeting 'hello' and fled into the bedroom muttering something about needing a shower.

Meanwhile, Wilson carried on a lengthy conversation with Taylor who was annoyed because small talk bored him. Wilson was impatient because he had expected an exclusive interview with Barbara Stanwyck. An hour passed. Taylor banged on the bedroom door and got no response. Wilson was embarrassed and the angry Taylor banged on the bedroom door again. Wilson finally left and devoted his column to Lieutenant Taylor and how rude Barbara had been. 'Did she need a shower *that* badly?'

Several nights later Barbara ran into Wilson at a nightclub. She approached him graciously and explained that she should never have agreed to an interview because Bob was in New York on official business. She did not want to overshadow him in any way. Wilson was so impressed by Barbara's humble explanation that he wrote a retraction and applauded her.

Taylor was sent to Illinois to await his discharge papers, and Stanwyck returned to Hollywood for *My Reputation* at Warner Brothers. One of her classier films, this was love story about a widow who falls in love with an Army major (George Brent). Her teenage sons and social circle do not approve of the widow's affair and do all they can to break it up. In the end, love reigns supreme. Coming across with a sincere warmth that was so unlike her real self, Stanwyck is the shy and righteous widow trying to satisfy everyone in her life. The film received mixed reviews, but was one of Barbara's personal favourites. *My Reputation* was released for viewing overseas before premiering in the United States.

Warner Brothers offered *Mildred Pierce* to Barbara who accepted with enthusiasm. She was eager to dig her teeth into the part of Mildred, a dowdy housewife who goes into the restaurant business and makes a fortune, but is ridiculed by her ungrateful daughter who has an affair with Mildred's selfish second husband. However, after many script revisions, producer Jerry Wald was tempted by Joan Crawford's offer to test for the lead role. She was so good he forgot about Stanwyck who said, 'I desperately wanted the part. I went after it. I knew what a great role for a woman it was, and I knew I could handle every facet of Mildred. I laid my cards on the table with Jerry Wald. After all, I had done a dozen pictures at Warner's. I paid my dues. I felt Mildred was me.'

Joan Crawford got the part and won an Oscar. Barbara was very disappointed, but she felt Joan deserved it.

Stanwyck's next film was *The Bride Wore Boots*, a light comedy with Robert Cummings and eight-year-old Natalie Wood. Barbara plays a horsewoman whose husband hates horses. They divorce, but reconcile after he rides an old nag to victory in a cup race.

Director Irving Pichel had done 13 takes of the hilarious steeplechase and told the riders, including Cummings, to prepare for a 14th, despite the intense heat. After the ASPCA replaced the horses, suddenly there was a dead silence as Stanwyck walked slowly across the grass to face the director. 'Mr Pichel,' she said in a loud voice, 'if Bob Cummings rides that race once more, you will never direct me in another scene!' She stared at him for one stern minute, then turned and took the long walk back to her trailer. Pichel used the prints he already had and shut down production for the day.

The New York Times review of *The Bride Wore Boots* was not a good one. 'It is a dull and depressing film. It is also a full-scale exhibition of the wastage of a competent star. Foolish lines so hopelessly hobble Barbara Stanwyck, that she should seek reparation from the courts. Robert Cummings should appeal for a judicial stay.'

It's not that Barbara had bad taste in choosing good films. She wanted to do *Jezebel* that earned Bette Davis an Oscar. And she had fought for *Mildred Pierce*. Now she set her sights on Ayn Rand's *The Fountainhead*. Warner Brothers bought the rights to the book with the idea of pairing Barbara with Humphrey Bogart. While Rand worked on the screenplay of her best-seller, Stanwyck made *The Strange Love of Martha Ivers* with Kirk Douglas, making his screen debut, and Van Heflin, who had won an Oscar for Best Supporting Actor in *Johnny Eager*. Douglas had heard wonderful things about working with Barbara, but she was indifferent to him. A few weeks later she complimented him on his acting. Douglas retorted, 'Too late, Miss Stanwyck.' Years later he said, 'She had no idea what I meant. But after that she was nice to me and we became friends.'

As Martha Ivers, Barbara is a heartless vixen who, as a teenager, murdered her wealthy aunt. The only witness was Kirk

Douglas. He marries Martha for power and money. She marries him to keep his mouth shut, and an innocent man is hanged. He thrives on liquor and she thrives on Van Heflin. In similar fashion to *Double Indemnity*, Kirk and Barbara kill each other in the end. *The Strange Love of Martha Ivers* was popular with the critics and at the box office.

CHAPTER ELEVEN

Undercurrent

On 5 November 1946, Robert Taylor was discharged from the Navy as a Senior Grade Lieutenant. He returned to MGM, but in his absence Van Johnson, Peter Lawford, Cornel Wilde and Frank Sinatra had been given the choice roles. Gary Cooper and John Wayne had also maintained their popularity.

'I didn't know what depression was until 1946,' Taylor said. He spent his days off hunting with Clark Gable, who was suffering from the same post-war slump. He told Bob, 'Mayer gives me Greer Garson in a thing called *Adventure*, and comes up with the slogan "Gable's back and Garson's got him!"'

One critic said, 'She can have him!'

Before Taylor went into the service, he was given a 20-year contract with MGM for $4,000 a week. When he got out of the Navy he did not ask for a raise because of taxes. Instead, the studio gave him a $75,000 twin-engine Beechcraft that he named 'Missy', Barbara's nickname, and hired his Navy buddy Ralph Couser as his co-pilot.

Tom Purvis, who lived in Illinois, accepted Taylor's invitation to visit him in Hollywood, but Barbara complained, 'Don't ever want to be a house guest and don't ever want a house guest!' Purvis found himself in a luxury hotel suite. 'Bob was embarrassed because I wasn't invited to stay at his place,' Tom said. 'He joked about Barbara buying a smaller house when he was away and they were building another bedroom. He slept in the sewing room. I didn't see much of Barbara. She didn't like me and I didn't like her. Just as well I didn't stay with them because she was always yelling at Bob and he never fought back.'

Unhappy at MGM and at home, Taylor, who loved good food, would fly to Palm Springs for lunch, to San Francisco for dinner or to New Orleans for some exotic food at Antoines, or to Oregon to fish for steelhead trout or to Texas to hunt quail.

'Bob is likely to stay up in his plane and never come down,' Barbara said in an interview. 'He can do anything a bird does but sit on a barbed wire fence! I think he's changed since he's been in the Navy.'

While Taylor co-starred with Katharine Hepburn in *Undercurrent*, Stanwyck made her first film in colour, *California*, at Paramount, and three pictures at Warner Brothers – *The Other Love* with David Niven, *The Two Mrs Carrolls* with Humphrey Bogart, and *Cry Wolf* with Errol Flynn.

MGM threw Bob a crumb – *The High Wall* – that went unnoticed until he made headlines when he testified before a visiting subcommittee of the House of Un-American Activities Committee inquiring into Communist activity in Hollywood. As a result, he volunteered to testify in Washington.

When Robert Stripling, chief committee investigator, asked, 'How long have you been employed as an actor?' laughter almost drowned out the reply of 'Since 1934'.

Question: Have you found considerable Communists or

fellow travellers asserting influence over the movies?

Answer: I have been looking for Communists for a long time. I have seen more indications recently, especially in the preparations of scripts. I've seen things that appear on the 'pink' side.

Question: Does any element in the Screen Actors' Guild follow the Communists' line?

Answer: Yes, sir, I must admit I have seen this. I am a member of the Board of Directors and it seems that at the general membership meetings, certain people, if not Communists, seem to be working awfully hard to be one.

Question: Do they have a disrupting influence?

Answer: On issues in which there is considerable agreement, certain persons 'stare' – not seemingly to understand. Howard Da Silva and actress Karen Morley are among those who disrupt things at the meetings. They, among others, ask questions and keep the sessions running to one or two o'clock in the morning.

Several senators predicted Taylor would face ridicule and the smear tactics of Communists as a result of his appearance that day.

'It doesn't bother me,' Bob said. 'Anytime the left-wing groups ridicule me, I take it as a compliment.'

Because Taylor was almost trampled to death by fans and female admirers, the court ordered more policemen on duty the following day when Robert Montgomery, Gary Cooper and Ronald Reagan were scheduled to testify.

Taylor was a hero at the time but he would be severely criticised by liberals in years to come.

In February 1947, Barbara and Bob took a three-week vacation in Europe. Much of their trip was highly publicised, but the press did not hint that this holiday was to salvage what was left of their marriage.

Helen Ferguson said, 'Barbara desperately wanted to hold on to Bob. His eyes were roving even in her presence these days, but I doubt he was aware of it. The vacation was her idea and I thought she was very brave considering her fear of travelling, even with Bob. Then it occurred to me that one of Barbara's films, *The Other Love*, was going to premiere in London at the same time. Maybe Bob didn't care, but I felt she should have devoted herself to him completely.'

The Taylors had reserved a grand suite at the Hotel George V in Paris, but reporters did not see them arrive in France or check into the hotel. The famous couple had literally disappeared. Four days later, Barbara, suffering from a bad cold, was staying at the American Hospital in Neuilly. An MGM press agent said, 'There was not adequate heat at the hotel and Miss Stanwyck decided to stay at the hospital rather than risk pneumonia. Bob is in Paris. His wife meets him there for dinner occasionally, but returns to her hospital bed to sleep.' A French reporter wanted to know why Barbara didn't snuggle up to Bob if there was no heat in the hotel. Before the press could find out more about their unusual living arrangements, the Taylors were seen at the Folies Bergère. Unfortunately, Barbara made a fool of herself by saying she was shocked to see so many showgirls prancing around wearing little more than a piece of chiffon. Had she forgotten that she had stripped down to nothing on stage in the Zeigfeld Shadowgraph number? To further insult the French, Barbara criticised American women who were buying clothes in Paris. 'It's unfair,' she said.

Stanwyck felt well enough to accompany Bob to Holland and Belgium, and then to London for the premiere of *The Other Love* in Leicester Square. On the red carpet they were mobbed by hundreds of fans. Police had to hoist Taylor on their shoulders, but he made light of it. 'Hell, I've been stripped down to my shorts in Times Square,' he laughed. 'I've had to walk down fire escapes without my shoes, and ride down freight elevators in white tie and tails.' He did, however, get a black eye in the crush. Headlines in the morning paper read: 'MOB SHINES ROBERT TAYLOR!' The joke around Hollywood was, 'Since when is Barbara a mob?'

The Taylors sailed home on the *S.S. America*. Barbara suffered with seasickness and was annoyed by Europeans on board who complained about the service. 'When American troops were going overseas not long ago, we didn't hear any of you complaining about the service,' she exclaimed. 'You were pretty damn happy to see American troops when they liberated Paris!'

Relieved to see the New York City skyline, Barbara, clinging to Bob's arm, disembarked only to be met by reporters who wanted to know if she was going to see Frank Fay in his smash Broadway play, *Harvey*. 'Not likely,' she snapped. 'I saw all the rabbits Frank Fay had to offer a long time ago!'

Helen Ferguson said, 'I met Barbara and Bob in New York. She wanted to continue on to California right away but I insisted they see at least one Broadway show. I arranged for them to see Maurice Chevalier's evening of *Songs and Impressions*. We enjoyed it and were invited backstage to join Chevalier in his dressing room. We waited a long time and when he showed up, he completely ignored us. Barbara turned purple. Bob grabbed her and left. All the way to the hotel he ranted and raved while Barbara wept. It was very embarrassing.'

The Taylors took the 20th Century Limited train to Chicago where Bob's plane was waiting. He flew on ahead and met Barbara's train in Los Angeles.

She was happy to be home and very excited about playing the feisty and selfish Dominque Francon in *The Fountainhead*. 'I saw myself as this woman who was rich and spoiled and refused to be dominated,' Barbara said. 'But when Warners assigned King Vidor to direct the movie, his idea of casting was completely different. He didn't think I was sexy enough to play the part.' He chose newcomer Patricia Neal instead.

Stanwyck was livid. On 21 June 1948, she sent Jack Warner a telegram. She reminded him that she had brought *The Fountainhead* to his attention and everyone assumed she would be in the picture. 'And now I find out that someone else is definitely playing the role. Naturally, Jack, I am bitterly disappointed.

'However, I can realistically see your problems, and based on all the circumstances it would appear to be to our mutual advantage to terminate our personal contractual relationship. I would appreciate hearing from you.'

Jack Warner replied, 'Since our actions have offended you and you desire to terminate your contract with us, it may be that, under the circumstances, this would be the best thing to do.'

Patricia Neal had a serious love affair with her married co-star, Gary Cooper, in the film, and aborted his baby. She was 22, he was 47. Cooper left his wife but changed his mind about getting a divorce. Neal married writer Roald Dahl in 1953 and won an Oscar for *Hud* in 1964. The following year she had several strokes, but survived and valiantly fought to regain her health and resume her career.

For *B.F.'s Daughter* at MGM, Barbara cut her shoulder-length hair, but refused to touch up the white streaks at her temples. Not only did her hairdresser suggest dyeing them, so did her friends. 'I'm forty-one,' she laughed. 'So what? If I'm destined to have prematurely white hair, so be it. I have no intention of lying about my age nor do I have any intention of going through that tedious job of having my hair coloured every week. I couldn't go through that.'

In *B.F.'s Daughter* she looked her age as the daughter of an influential father, played by Charles Coburn. She marries a intellectual (Van Heflin) and uses her power and money to further his career. Unfortunately, the critics compared J.P. Marquand's novel *B.F's Daughter* to the film that toned down the snobbish and spoiled rich, but Stanwyck and Heflin were praised for their fine adaptation of the characters.

During production of the classic *Sorry, Wrong Number*, Barbara's hair turned completely white. *Life* magazine described her part of an invalid, played mostly in bed, as 'the most extended emotional jag in recent movie history'. It was a choice role and Stanwyck was eager to do it, but confessed it was exhausting. 'For twelve straight days I had to be on an emotional high, playing a bedridden woman and knowing someone is going to murder me. I lived the part, but can you imagine how hard it was to leave the studio each night in a high state of anxiety and terror, go home and eat and sleep and get up the next day to start all over again?'

Barbara was living the role of the neurotic lady dialling the telephone frantically for help. Finally, she asked director Anatole Litvak if he could arrange a filming schedule so that she could do the terrifying scenes consecutively, and he complied.

Cue magazine said, 'For sheer, unadulterated terror there have been few films in recent years to match the quivering fright of *Sorry, Wrong Number* – and few performances to equal the hysteria-ridden picture of a woman doomed, as portrayed by Barbara Stanwyck.

'Miss Stanwyck gives one of the finest performances of her

career – a carefully calculated, skillfully integrated picture of developing psychological terror that provides a filmic highlight of the year.'

Barbara was nominated for another Academy Award – her fourth. 'I will not win this year for best actress,' she told a reporter, 'because I haven't been nominated enough. Only four times! If I get nominated next year, they'll have to give me the door prize, won't they? At least the bride should throw me the bouquet.

'Not that I wouldn't like to have an Oscar, but I've lost three times before and it's hard to get your expectations up and not win. It's bad luck to discuss it. Besides, I feel Olivia de Havilland really deserves it for *The Snake Pit*.' Other actresses nominated were Irene Dunne in *I Remember Mama*, Jane Wyman for *Johnny Belinda*, and Ingrid Bergman in *Joan of Arc*.

Barbara went to the Oscar ceremonies in a frustrated mood, knowing that she had been nominated four times, but her peers had voted for someone else. She lost this time to Jane Wyman, who as a deaf mute had no lines in *Johnny Belinda*.

Occasionally the Oscar race is a popularity contest and sometimes it's based on sentiment. Elizabeth Taylor was nominated in 1958 for *Cat on a Hot Tin Roof* and in 1959 for *Suddenly Last Summer*, two of her most outstanding performances, but when Taylor broke up Eddie Fisher's marriage to Debbie Reynolds, she was ostracised by Hollywood. After her marriage to Fisher, she nearly died from pneumonia in London and was welcomed back with an Oscar for the mediocre *Butterfield 8*.

Bette Davis was nominated ten times for Best Actress but won only twice. She was very difficult to work with and unfriendly off the movie set.

Elected officials to the Academy of Motion Picture Arts and

Sciences determine Oscar nominations. All members vote the final awards. The movie studios at this time wagered campaigns and gave lavish parties for their contract players who were nominated for the covetous awards. Mingling with the right people was an advantage, but Barbara refused to play the game.

Taylor found adjusting to civilian life difficult. He didn't appreciate the phoniness in Hollywood either. 'I was better off financially when I was drawing a lieutenant's pay than before or after the war,' he commented. 'Barbara and I were left with $5,000 a year between us when I was earning comparatively nothing. She was able to divide her income between us for taxation. But I guess she's rather have me home and pay . . .'

When asked by a friend about the trip to Europe Bob replied, 'I don't know why the hell people think they can save a marriage by getting on a boat for a change of scenery when the change of scenery is each other.'

Despite her hectic schedule, Barbara was forced to take a solid look at her marriage. Helen Ferguson advised her. 'Try to be a good sport with Bob. Try to share some of his hobbies if it kills you.'

'It probably will,' she said.

Barbara referred to Bob's plane as 'the crate', and she had yet to go near it. 'He flew the damn thing from Los Angeles to New Orleans and back by way of Denver just to test a new radio,' she remarked with a tone of resentment. But the time had come for her to make some long overdue sacrifices for her husband. She agreed to take a ride in his plane. Bob called friends to tell them Barbara was actually going to fly with him. The drive to the airport was a quiet one. When she spotted 'the crate', she began trembling, but got aboard. In the air Stanwyck was petrified, holding on to the seat with both hands. She was pale and ill when they landed in Palm Springs an hour later. Taylor considered this the greatest gift she had ever given him and talked about it for weeks.

'Barbara saw a change in Bob,' Helen Ferguson said. 'She finally realised what it took to save the marriage so she decided to go on a camping trip with Bob, Gary Cooper and Ernest Hemingway.' She naturally thought having 'Coop' along would give her a chance to chat about old times, but he was different in the woods. Like Bob, he forgot about the movie business and concentrated on the hunt. Taylor was impressed with Hemingway, but Hemingway was not impressed with Taylor. He liked Barbara who wasn't impressed at all. When she got home, her only comment was, 'Never again!' She could not understand how he could spend days planning a fishing trip, get all enthused, and run out of the house with a truckload of gear only to come back and leave dozens of dead fish on the back porch. 'He rarely cooked them. The smell was awful. All that planning and excitement for nothing but a lotta stink.'

Once Barbara had a party and 'allowed' Bob to invite his cronies. John Wayne was there and said she retired early. 'We were just a bunch of guys telling tall tales about the big fish we didn't catch and the bears that got too close to our tents, when she appeared in a nightgown at the top of the stairs and yelled, 'Get up here to bed where you belong!' I can't repeat what else she said but it had to do with sex and what she wanted him to do. I might have told her where a wife belonged and how she should act, but I knew she would take it out on Bob. I felt very bad for him. What happened that night got around Hollywood like a tornado.'

CHAPTER TWELVE

Showdown

Barbara's efforts to salvage what was left of her marriage by sharing Bob's hobbies did not begin to solve their problems. Although he was not aware of it at the time, Taylor found himself with two mothers and was unable to perform with Barbara in bed. 'I've got a prostate problem,' he lied, trying to stall for time. Barbara became suspicious. If a man wasn't satisfied at home, he must be going elsewhere, but there was no evidence whatsoever that Bob was seeing another woman. Not even the customary rumours. Thinking it over logically, Barbara came to her own conclusion. If he wasn't sleeping with her or another woman he had to be a homosexual. The more she thought about it the more is made sense. She accused him of being gay.

Bob had been an exciting lover before going into the service, but when he came home he brought Ralph Couser, his co-pilot, with him. The two men worked together at MGM, flew his plane everywhere together and shared other mutual interests. Bob's other buddies did not telephone him at home but Couser did.

Taylor ignored Barbara's insinuations because he understood her frustrations. There were more accusations and more fighting. She confronted Bob about his 'affair' with Couser. He said nothing. It was too degrading for a response. His indifference enraged Barbara, who continued to nag. When Couser called, she announced sarcastically, 'Hey, Bob, your wife's on the phone!'

Taylor took it and much more.

Convinced he was losing his virility or maybe his interest in women, Bob went to a psychologist, who had known Bob socially for years and was acquainted with his mother and Barbara.

'When Bob was a little boy,' the doctor explained, 'his mother dressed him up in frilly clothes and she fawned over his gorgeous looks. Before he signed with MGM, he took acting lessons at the Pasadena Playhouse whose founder Gilmore Brown was a homosexual. Bob was not sophisticated enough for Brown who pursued him anyway. Harry Hay, a radical homosexual was a student also and the one who spread rumours about Bob and Brown having an affair. Bob was signed by MGM, became a star and was labelled 'Pretty Boy'. He never forgot this so when Barbara accused him of being gay, Bob thought this might be true. Most upsetting was his rocky marriage. He did not want to be just another movie star getting a divorce, but could Barbara ever again arouse him?

'I knew we had to eliminate the homosexual stigma first,' continued the psychologist, 'so I asked him if he had been attracted to any woman lately. He said, "I get a goddam hot sensation in my groin when I see a sexy looking woman."'

'I told him a few things straight from the shoulder both as a friend and as a doctor. He was not gay. I was sure of that. Then I explained my concept of his having two mothers. Men do not get the urge to go to bed with their mothers. Taking it from there, the only way to prove that he was *not* a homosexual was to see other women, and not to worry about his marriage until he regained confidence in himself.'

A few months later Bob told the doctor he was seeing his leading lady in *The Bribe*. Twenty-six-year-old Ava Gardner was labelled by the press as 'the most beautiful animal in the world'. She had the face of an angel and the body of a goddess. Ava had been married and divorced from Mickey Rooney and Artie Shaw, and would marry Frank Sinatra in 1952. In her memoirs she had nothing but praise for Bob and how beautiful their affair was. Occasionally they went to his mother's house in the afternoons to avoid being seen at a hotel. Bob said that he and Ava were having great sex with no commitments. He seldom saw Barbara who was busy with her career, although she managed to find time for William Holden, who was separated from his wife. Stanwyck either began or resumed the affair with her 'golden boy'.

Taylor was adamant about saving his marriage, however. He told the doctor, 'I'm sure we can work it out. I hope so.'

During the late forties, Barbara's films were going from bad to worse. In *The Lady Gambles* she portrays a housewife who gets casino fever in Las Vegas and ends up in a mental ward. Robert Preston is her sympathetic husband. It was not a quality picture, but critics agreed that Stanwyck did her usual capable job. *The Lady Gambles* was considered a 'dud'.

East Side, West Side at MGM was not much better. James Mason was cast as Barbara's husband who is torn between her and another woman portrayed by none other than Ava Gardner! Did Barbara know that Ava was the other woman in her personal life as well? If so, there were no incidents during production. The nervous actress in *East Side, West Side* was Nancy Davis, who was making her third picture. It was director Mervyn LeRoy who introduced her to actor Ronald Reagan whom she would marry. In 1980 she moved into the White House for eight years after 'Ronnie' was elected President of the United States. Robert Taylor was Reagan's best friend.

In *The File on Thelma Jordon*, Barbara takes on the title role of a scheming woman on trial for murder. This film moved at such a slow pace it was panned by critics who thought Barbara's acting was 'forced'.

No Man of Her Own with John Lund is the story of an unwed pregnant woman (Stanwyck) involved in a train crash. She is mistaken for the wife of a man killed in the wreck and is welcomed by his family. The truth comes out in the end but she finds happiness with the dead man's brother. *The New York Times* said the film was 'diversion for none but the suckers'. *The Times* also commented on the state of Barbara's career: 'Along with Bette Davis and Joan Crawford, she is one of the steadiest sufferers on the screen. Seems like every time Miss Stanwyck makes a picture she makes a false-step – fictionally speaking, that is. People know what to expect.'

Barbara rushed into *The Furies* at Paramount. She is the strong-willed daughter of Walter Huston, a self-made cattle king of the old West, and owner of a ranch bearing the name of 'The Furies'. When Huston refused to relinquish land he wrested from squatters, Barbara sides with the people he has wronged. The film offered outstanding scenery, plenty of action and romance. Stanwyck and co-stars Wendell Corey, Gilbert Roland and Judith Anderson are superb. But it was Huston's picture – and his last. He died before *The Furies* was released.

In November 1949, a beautiful 17-year-old actress sighed, 'This is the day I grew up! I started working on *Conspirator* and no one can say I'm a child in this picture because I am playing Robert

Taylor's wife. He is just as wonderful as everyone in Hollywood said he was. I have to admit I got nervous when he took me in his arms and made love to me.'

Elizabeth Taylor was studying her algebra when she was called to the set. She powdered her nose and dabbed perfume behind each ear. As for her 38-year old co-star, he was calm and understanding until he realised the 'little girl' wasn't so little after all. 'She was stacked,' he told Tom Purvis. 'I didn't realise it until she appeared in a negligée. It was one of the few times in my life I couldn't control myself. I got a hard-on and couldn't stand up. I motioned to the cameraman and whispered my problem in his ear so he focused on me from the waist up. I spent the entire day in that condition. I sure as hell wasn't going to try to seduce a seventeen-year-old. I might have tried a few years later when we did *Ivanhoe*, but she was chasing after Michael Wilding and wasn't interested in anyone else.'

When Taylor returned to Hollywood, Louis B. Mayer told him to pack for Italy to film *Quo Vadis?* with Deborah Kerr and Peter Ustinov.

Barbara's last in a rapid succession of movies was *To Please a Lady* with Clark Gable. He is a racing driver and she plays a snobbish newspaper columnist who writes a scathing article that results in his being banned from racing. Stanwyck and Gable work well together and their characters were evenly matched – tough! Twenty years earlier he had slapped her face in *Night Nurse* and she gets the same treatment in *To Please a Lady*:

> *Clark*: You'd better listen to what I'm saying or I'll knock
>   that smile off your face.
> *Barbara*: Knock it off!

He does and she comes back for more. The picture was a hit.

In an interview with gossip columnist Louella Parsons, Barbara admitted there had been some unhappiness in her marriage to Taylor. 'It began when he bought that airplane,' she explained. 'He was always on some kind of hunting or fishing trip with his friends. I asked Bob if he wanted me to make fewer films and he insisted I continue working.'

Louella wanted to know how she felt about Bob's being in Italy for six months. 'I'm lonely for him,' Barbara replied. 'I'm planning to spend a few months with him in Rome. When you've been married happily for ten years, you miss seeing him around.'

Cheerfully Barbara said she wanted to visit friends in Paris and London before going on to Rome. But in the summer of 1950, rumours were flying from the Italian capital to the movie capital. Barbara usually ignored exaggerated tales, but the stories about Bob and a bit player, 25-year-old Lia De Leo, came from a reliable source – MGM's hairdresser to the stars, Sidney Guilaroff. He claimed Stanwyck asked him to 'keep an eye on Bob'.

Helen Ferguson explained, 'Barbara called me one night and said, "I'm going to Rome and you're going with me!" So I began packing.'

Stanwyck was being considered for the lead in *All About Eve*, but she wanted to work near Bob and decided to make *Another Man's Poison* in London. The script was being written exclusively for her. She had originally planned to travel by boat to England, make the movie, surprise Bob in Rome, return to London for retakes and sail back to New York with him. But the threat of Lia De Leo changed all that.

Though it's difficult to think of anyone other than Bette Davis playing the ageing actress Margo Channing in *All About*

Eve, Barbara would have handled the role beautifully, but the timing was all wrong. This sacrifice came too late to save her marriage, but she surely could have given her career a boost. Margo's best speech about women who favour the limelight over marriage could have been written for Barbara – 'Funny business, a woman's career. The things you drop on your way up the ladder – so you can move faster – you forget you'll need them when you go back to being a woman. That's one career all females have in common whether we like it or not. Being a woman. Sooner or later we have to work at it, no matter what other careers we've had or wanted. And in the last analysis nothing is any good unless you can look up just before dinner – or turn in bed – and there he is. Without that you're not a woman. You're someone with a French provincial office – or a book full of clippings. But you're not a woman. Slow curtain. The end.'

Barbara had not been considered for the part of Norma Desmond in *Sunset Boulevard*, but she envied Gloria Swanson who played the washed-up actress. Bill Holden was cast as the young writer who meets her and says, 'You're Norma Desmond. You used to be in silent pictures. You used to be big.'

She responds, ' I *am* big. It's the *pictures* that got small.'

Barbara went to the screening of *Sunset Boulevard* with Holden and did everything but bow down and kiss Gloria Swanson's feet. One observer referred to it as a 'public homage'.

Holden was nominated for Best Actor and lost, but took home an Oscar in 1954 for *Stalag 17*. He owed it all to Barbara.

MGM announced that Barbara Stanwyck was taking a vacation to be with Taylor for six weeks, and 'she eagerly awaited the chance to sightsee in such a beautiful country.'

Helen Ferguson thought Barbara put up a magnificent front. 'She was sick and afraid on the flights to Rome. Not only was sitting on a plane tearing her nerves to shreds, but the thought that her husband was openly having an affair at the destination was shattering. But Bob met us warmly and seemed genuinely happy to see Barbara.'

The press watched the Taylors carefully. MGM officials made certain there was no adverse publicity and concentrated on Bob showing Barbara the traditional sights of Rome. Helen tried to cover up the tension by emphasising how happy Barbara was to see her husband and that Bob was 'tickled pink' to have her in Rome.

The inevitable happened. Barbara wanted to know what was going on. Who was Lia De Leo? What was going on between them? Why was he flaunting the affair? Was it serious?

Bob denied the relationship. He was under a great deal of pressure doing *Quo Vadis?* It was the most expensive film ever produced at that time – $7 million. Was he going to lock himself in his apartment every night? 'Of course I go out. Is there a crime in that?' he asked. 'Ask Tom Purvis. He was here for two weeks.'

Barbara smirked. 'What kind of fool do you think I am?'

If she had been on friendly terms with Purvis he might have helped her through the dilemma. 'Bob and I spent our nights together in different restaurants eating stuff we never heard of. He had a chef so sometimes we'd have dinner in his apartment. On one occasion a girl called from the lobby and said she was coming up, but he wanted me to stay while she was there. Bob told me she was an aspiring actress and it might give the wrong impression if he were alone with her. At the time I was sure there was nothing going on between them.'

The psychologist who helped Taylor through his fear of homosexuality commented on the showdown in Rome. 'Bob's personality was remarkable. He could take a good deal of harassment and never speak up. But everyone has a breaking point and Bob had his in Rome. Barbara accused him of having many affairs and when he didn't react, she harped on Lia De Leo, but still Bob remained silent. Then Barbara threatened divorce, ripping into his affair with the Italian girl. Bob exploded, *"At least I can get it up with her!"'*

'I'll bleed you for the rest of your life,' she said.

Barbara left Rome immediately. Her plans to make a film in London were cancelled. She told the producer, 'My whole life has fallen apart. I can't think of anything else right now. Filing for divorce will take everything out of me, but it has to be done.'

In September 1950 Stanwyck sailed on the *Queen Elizabeth* and bravely faced reporters. 'Rome wasn't great,' she said. 'They were shooting scenes with lions and bulls and everything smelled awful.' When asked about Taylor, she managed a weak smile and said, 'Being with Bob is always wonderful.'

In November Taylor finished *Quo Vadis?* and was preparing to leave his apartment for the airport. When he appeared in the lobby with his luggage, Lia was waiting and took him by surprise. She flung herself into his arms, covering his face with kisses while photographers took pictures.

Bob gently but firmly pushed her away and hurried to the limousine. Lia did not follow him because she was ready to make a statement to the press. She said she was 'Robert Taylor's big love' – and had been throughout the filming of *Quo Vadis?* 'He is tired of her (Barbara) and he told me so,' Lia said.

Taylor refused comment at the airport and returned to Hollywood where pictures of him and Lia were on the front pages. Gossip columnists hinted that the Taylors had separated, but a few days after Bob got home, he and Barbara went to San Francisco together. Later it was revealed that Taylor entered a hospital there to have an operation to remove a double hernia. Barbara remained by his side and called Louella Parsons. 'Those hours that Bob was on the operating table were the worst I have ever spent in my life.'

'What are your future plans,' Parsons asked tactfully.

Barbara said they were taking a vacation together, but instead he went to Palm Springs and she went into hiding at the home of friends in Hollywood.

The divorce announcement was made on 16 December 1950, through their press agents. Helen Ferguson broke down in tears and handed the paper to Howard Strickling, head of MGM publicity.

The Taylors issued a joint statement:

In the past few years, because of professional requirements, we have been separated just too often and too long. Our sincere and continued efforts to maintain our marriage have failed. We are deeply disappointed that we could not solve our problems. We really tried. We unhappily and reluctantly admit what we have denied even to our closest friends because we wanted to work things out together in as much privacy as possible. There will be a California divorce. Neither of us has any other romantic interest whatsoever.

CHAPTER THIRTEEN

He Loves Me.
He Loves Me Not

Louella Parsons wrote in her column, 'It is almost certain that the Italian girl had nothing to do with the Taylors' decision to part. Trouble started long before Bob went to Rome. I spoke to Barbara and I am inclined to think when they decided to end their marriage it came suddenly. It was Bob, however, who asked for his freedom.'

In another interview a reporter reminded Barbara that her marriage to Bob was often pointed out as the one perfect example that two famous film stars could have separate careers and a happy marriage, too.

'That was the damn trouble!' Barbara exclaimed. 'Separate careers! We have been separated too much! I was a long-distance, telephone wife. Bob and I could never get together. When I was in a picture, he was on vacation. When I was off for a few weeks, he was sent somewhere halfway around the world. The best we could do was shake hands at the door as we went in and out.'

On 21 February 1951, looking chic in a slim toast-coloured

suit with a matching hat topping off her grey and white curls, Barbara Stanwyck told the court in a three-minute hearing (one of the shortest divorces on record) that her husband, Robert Taylor, was tired of being married and wanted to be a bachelor again.

'He said he enjoyed his freedom during the months he was making a movie in Italy,' she testified. 'He wanted to be able to live his life without restrictions. I was very shocked and very grieved over it and was quite ill. For several weeks I was under the care of my physician.'

Barbara's witness, Helen Ferguson, testified that she received an urgent and hysterical telephone call from her friend to come right over to the Taylor house. 'When I got there, I found Barbara in a tragic emotional state. She said she was going to give Bob the freedom he wanted.'

The judge said, 'That will be enough. Divorce granted.'

Barbara asked the court for permission to drop the surname Taylor and she was awarded their $100,000 house, all furnishings and 15 per cent of Taylor's earnings until she remarried or either party died.

As she was leaving court, Barbara refused to comment on rumours that her matinee idol husband wanted his freedom because he had fallen in love with an Italian actress. 'I don't know,' she said with a crooked smile. 'You'll have to ask Mr Taylor about that!' Then she was asked if she had a new boyfriend. Barbara widened her eyes and shuddered. 'Oh, no, I've had enough. I don't want any more of that!'

In later years Barbara said, 'I don't want someone who doesn't want me. There's the door. You can open it. That's all you have to do. If you can't open it, I'll open it for you.'

Shortly after Stanwyck went to court, the shapely Italian bit player held a press conference. The headline read:

BOB'S BIG LOVE SEES NO HITCH IN HER PLANS

Rome: Redheaded Lia De Leo, for whose love Robert Taylor ostensibly broke up with Barbara Stanwyck, today was so little impressed with the 'great lover' of American films that she indicated she would rather remain good friends with Taylor than marry him. She admitted she was Bob's true love when he was in Rome, but marriage did not seem to be on the cards, though 'If it depended on him alone, I'm sure we would marry.' She said the break-up of Taylor's marriage was inevitable: 'I knew this would happen ever since he was here. He was tired of his wife and he told me so. It was evident that, after meeting me, a divorce was the only possible solution.'

Lia posed in a striped bathing suit that showed every curve to its best advantage.

Reporters hounded Taylor. Once, while having cocktails with Rex Harrison, he uncharacteristically blew up over persistent questions about Lia. 'What about her?' he snapped. 'I'm here, aren't I? Is she with me?'

When asked about his social life, he said, 'What about it? I've nothing to hide. My life's an open book. In fact everybody's getting into the act. I've read so many stories about myself that half the time I can't keep up with what I'm doing – or rather what I'm supposed to be doing.'

Barbara moved out of the house she shared with Bob almost immediately after they parted. She auctioned off most of the furniture. Among the items were paintings, one of them a Renoir, and a series of pioneering women by Fredric Remington. Barbara's bed sold for $360, and Taylor's laced leather headboard and end table built into it, including a wooden horse supporting a lamp, sold for $630.

Two days after the auction, Barbara and Bob were seen dining at Ciro's in Hollywood. Bubbling and radiant, she smiled when reporters approached. 'There's no use keeping it a secret,' she sighed. 'I'm carrying a torch for Bob, but it's too early to say whether we will be reconciled.' Barbara confided this was her second date with Taylor since the divorce decree that would not become final for a year. He said nothing but the ebullient Barbara made up for that. 'There will be no other man in my life,' she told reporters. When Stanwyck spoke these words – words that she would repeat for a lifetime, it was pathetically convincing to even the most persistent sceptic.

Taylor was sincerely trying to recapture what he and Barbara had when they were courting. He hoped that champagne, roses, romantic music, and dancing might bring them closer together. He would be true to himself and 'try like hell' to rekindle the flame.

Barbara admitted to Bob that she only tried to frighten him – to bring him to his senses by threatening divorce. She was stunned when he agreed and although she was not one to forgive and forget, she would 'just this once'.

Bob's psychologist said, 'Bob didn't want to lose Barbara because no man wants to lose his mother. He was determined to change this image of her to one of wife and lover, but it couldn't be. He would have to let her go if for no other reason than sparing Barbara more pain. I told him what he really wanted was her forgiveness, not a reconciliation. He disagreed with me because leaving the nest wasn't easy for him.'

Taylor began dating other women discreetly. One of his favourite girlfriends was the honey blonde actress, Virginia Grey. She had been Clark Gable's favourite for seven years and it was assumed they would marry, but in a drunken state he eloped with someone else. Bob always arranged a quiet evening at

Virginia's home in Encino, bringing with him steaks, wine and his favourite records. 'I took it for granted Bob did not want to be seen with a woman in public until his divorce was final,' Virginia said. 'How Barbara found out I will never know, but I learned the hard way that she resented any woman he dated.

In the fifties, the studio system was beginning to fade. When Louis B. Mayer was dethroned for being too old fashioned, Dory Schary took over command of MGM. The great stars demanded too much money and their contracts were not renewed. Lana Turner and Clark Gable were two of the most famous players who left the studio that once bragged they 'had more stars than there were in the heavens.' Others followed, but Taylor fared better than ever and became the screen's knight in shining armour in *Ivanhoe, Knights of the Round Table* and *Quentin Durwood* before terminating the longest running studio contract player in movie history – 24 years.

Barbara was struggling. She had seen the last of her great pictures though she would remain popular at the box office. Her first film after her marital split was *The Man With a Cloak*, a story set in 1848 New York. She plays a wealthy man's housekeeper scheming to get his money. Joseph Cotton, who turns out to be Edgar Allan Poe, is a mysterious stranger in a cloak helping the rightful heirs. Jim Backus, also in the film, called it a 'pretentious piece of merde (shit)'. The critics said *The Man With a Cloak* was a routine melodrama.

Stanwyck looked forward to *Clash by Night*, adapted from a play by Clifford Odets. She is excellent as the wife of a fisherman (Paul Douglas) who has an affair with a movie projectionist (Robert Ryan).

Marilyn Monroe, in one of her first important movie roles, was habitually late, nervous, unprepared and clumsy. Robert Ryan remembered, 'It upsets everyone's timing when someone doesn't show up on schedule and then stumbles and stammers. Paul and I were furious and ready to tell her exactly how we felt, but Marilyn was so innocent and angelic, we melted.'

Stanwyck had to put up with many retakes, but was patient with Marilyn because 'she couldn't get out of her own way. She wasn't disciplined and was often late, but she didn't do it viciously.'

Robert Slatzer, who wrote several books about Marilyn Monroe and claimed to be married to her briefly in October 1952, said Barbara was intimate with Marilyn, who was easily seduced if her career depended on it. 'Stanwyck took charge,' he said. 'She had no patience with actors who were as unprepared as Marilyn in *Clash by Night*. She said, "With a body like hers, she doesn't have to be a good actress." Marilyn thought it was an honour to have Barbara want her. She had nothing to lose by giving in.'

What bothered Stanwyck was the theme of the picture – a marriage almost destroyed by adultery. Fritz Lang, the director, understood the delicate subject of the film, which closely resembled Stanwyck's recent plight. 'One morning she came to me and complained about a particular scene because it was badly written,' Lang said. 'I knew the scene and thought it was very well written. I asked to speak frankly and she nodded. I told her I thought the scene reminded her of something that had happened in her own life and that was the reason she couldn't play it. Barbara looked at me and said, "You son of a bitch!", turned around and did the scene as written. We only had to do it once. Her line was, "People change. You find out what's important and what isn't. What you really want." '

Variety said, 'Miss Stanwyck plays the part with her customary defiance and sullenness.'

Barbara was pushing herself too hard during *Clash by Night*.

She was in poor health, but completed the film without telling anyone. Her resistance was very low and the day after the final scene was shot, she was rushed to the hospital with pneumonia.

During her brief recovery, Barbara agreed to do *Jeopardy* at MGM. The plot revolves around a family road trip to Mexico. Dad (Barry Sullivan) falls into a jetty to save his young son and is trapped by timbers. Mom (Barbara) sets out in the car for help and encounters an escaped convict. *The New York Times* wrote, 'Ralph Meeker as the desperado is the antithesis of his name. Only a scriptwriter could fancy Miss Stanwyck working him into the deal.'

Barbara continued to see Bob who gave her expensive birthday and Christmas presents. When he was on location making a film, he wrote and telephoned faithfully. He told reporters, 'Sure I plan to see Barbara and she's more beautiful than ever.' She was also upfront with the press: 'We are good friends again. We have dinner, go dancing and talk. Conjecture is the cheapest thing in the world. I know what I know and Bob knows what he knows. Other people do not.'

Taylor began dating other women openly when his divorce from Barbara became final in February 1952. He was linked to Eleanor Parker, the actress who complemented him most on the screen, but he told Purvis, 'She makes me nervous. She's too much like Barbara.' It was Parker who co-starred with Bob in *Above and Beyond*, the story of Colonel Tibbets, the pilot of the plane that dropped the atom bomb on Hiroshima. This was the closest Taylor got to being nominated for an Oscar.

Barbara had an affair of her own during production of *Titanic*, co-starring her good friend Clifton Webb, a distinguished homosexual, who said Stanwyck was his 'favourite lesbian'. Also in the film was 23-year-old Robert Wagner, who plays the young man in love with Stanwyck's daughter on board the ill-fated *Titanic*.

Wagner was born on 10 February 1930, in Detroit, Michigan, and his family moved to Los Angeles when he was seven. He worked as a caddy at the Bel-Air Country Club when he met many famous stars including Clark Gable. He was determined to get into the movies and had the good looks to succeed. *Titanic* was his tenth film. It not only helped his career, but had a great effect in his personal life as well. There were rumours of an affair between him and Stanwyck, but he denied it until after Barbara's death. During filming, he drove her home from a party and when he was unlocking her front door, he looked at her, '. . . and I saw something I hadn't seen in her eyes before. It was a magical look of interest . . . and appreciation . . . and desire,' he wrote. 'I took her into my arms and kissed her. I never had a reaction from a woman like that. A different kiss. A different feeling.' How did they manage to keep it out of the gossip columns? 'It was all handled,' Wagner said. 'We were very discreet. She was a sensitive lady beneath that tough outer shell. She changed my whole approach to my work, made me want to learn the business completely.'

In Wagner's book *Pieces of My Heart* he writes that Barbara cooked dinner for him often, which is something she never did for Taylor. He also confides she made regular visits to a man who gave her sodium pentothal because 'she had a lot of things going on in her head.' A sad revelation in his best-selling book was the small scar on Stanwyck's chest, a grim reminder of her affair with Jazz Singer Al Jolson who used her as an ashtray.

Wagner, who reminded Barbara of Taylor and was about the same age as when they met, claimed the affair lasted four years. He married Natalie Wood in 1957; they divorced in 1962 but remarried in 1972. She tragically drowned in 1981, off Santa

Catalina where their yacht *Spendor* was moored when he was starring in the popular TV series, *Hart to Hart*. He is currently married happily to actress Jill St John.

Titanic did not feature Barbara in as many scenes as she was accustomed to, but her role was dynamic and each time she appeared, it was a turning point in the story. Her final farewell to Clifton Webb as the ship is sinking is touching.

'The night we were filming the scene in the outdoor tank at 20th Century Fox, it was bitter cold,' Barbara related in a press interview. 'I was forty-seven feet up in a lifeboat swinging on the davits. The water below was agitated into a heaving rolling mass and it was thick with other lifeboats full of women and children. I looked down and thought: if one of those ropes snaps now it's goodbye for you. Then I looked up at the faces lining the rail, those left behind to die with the ship. I thought of the men and women who had been through this thing. We were recreating a real tragedy and I burst into tears. I shook with great racking sobs and couldn't stop.'

This vivid description was typical of Helen Ferguson's press releases, but there can be no doubt that Stanwyck felt the icy impact of the great ship as she filmed the tragic story of the mighty *Titanic*.

*

In Universal's *All I Desire*, Stanwyck takes the role of a wife and mother who deserts her family to pursue the stage. The story begins when she returns home 10 years later for her daughter's graduation, is reunited with her husband (Richard Carlson) and decides there's no place like home.

The New York Times said, 'Since Miss Stanwyck is an accomplished veteran she gives a better performance than could reasonably be expected under the enervating circumstances.'

Regarding *All I Desire*, Stanwyck said she played the part

many times, 'a bad woman trying to make up for past mistakes. But I like gutsy roles. I'd rather not act at all than do Pollyannas. I've got to play human beings. My only problem is finding a way to play my fortieth fallen female in a different way from the thirty-ninth.'

The Moonlighter, a western with Fred MacMurray was filmed in 3-D which is about all one can say about it. Gun toting Barbara battles it out with rustler MacMurray during their love-hate relationship. Either her marksmanship or her beauty impresses Fred and they ride off together into the sunset at the conclusion of what *The New York Times* called a 'sow's ear'.

Though Barbara had a stunt girl, she did most of the difficult scenes herself. One of them was sliding down a rocky waterfall into a hazardous river. She was known for her determination to undertake dangerous tasks. She became a stunt expert and loved these challenges that would eventually take their toll on her health, but she wanted to be part of the action rather than sit on the sidelines. She got her chance in *Blowing Wild* as a power-crazed woman who wants control of Mexican oil fields. She is married to one wildcatter (Anthony Quinn) and in love with another (Gary Cooper). Stanwyck is a psychotic tramp in this picture. She is so wicked that Cooper tries to choke her when he finds out she has killed his best friend. For realism, she told Cooper, 'Don't try to fake it. I want my eyes to pop out and the veins in my neck to swell.' In the struggle, Cooper got so carried away in his hatred of her (prompted by Barbara) that he did not hear the director yell, 'Cut!' twice. When Cooper finally let her go, she slumped to the ground and couldn't talk for two days.

Anthony Quinn watched Barbara and Gary playfully fondle each other on the grass during a long break in filming. 'They were hot and heavy,' he said, 'and I wondered why they didn't excuse themselves. They were all over each other. I honestly don't know what happened behind closed doors and I didn't care, but I was a little surprised at how blatant they were.'

The critics panned *Blowing Wild*, but moviegoers wanted to see Gary Cooper who won an Oscar for *High Noon* and Anthony Quinn who also won an Oscar for Best Supporting Actor in *Viva Zapata*. Barbara was disappointing in this picture. Her films were going from bad to worse.

CHAPTER FOURTEEN

Alone

On 23 May 1951, 27-year-old Ursula Schmidt-Hut Thiess arrived in the United States from Germany. She was divorced from actor-producer George Thiess. It was an unfortunate wartime union, but she bore him two children – first a daughter, Manuela, then a son, Michael. Working as a model, Ursula was discovered by Howard Hughes and her picture appeared on the cover of *Life* magazine. She was proclaimed 'The Most Beautiful Girl in the World'.

On 24 April 1952, her agent invited her out to dinner at the Coconut Grove with him, his wife and a blind date – Robert Taylor. Reporters were eagerly waiting when they left the nightclub, but Bob had no comment. A picture of the couple appeared in the newspaper the following day. One caption read, 'Bob Taylor is finally dating someone who is prettier than himself.'

Stanwyck tried to drown loneliness and frustrations with liquor. Those people in Hollywood who had little respect for her said she drank far too much and was attracted to the Taylor image – the clean, dimpled, boyish type with a trim body. Her adversaries referred to them as 'studs' and said she looked foolish flirting with them so openly. Though Barbara's heavy drinking did not affect her work, she made up for it at night. Uncle Buck was usually waiting for her with a stiff drink when she returned from the studio. She was carrying a heavy torch for Taylor whose official address was his mother's house, although he was living with Ursula. To avoid publicity and, his friends speculated, to avoid hurting or angering Barbara, he stayed home and enjoyed home-cooked meals. He told reporters, 'I am not engaged. I want to marry again, but I don't know when or to whom, but it would be a dismal prospect to be a bachelor for the rest of my life.'

'What about Miss Theiss?' they wanted to know.

'Ursula is truly lovely,' he replied. 'She has the most beautiful eyes I have ever seen. They're brown with specks of gold. And her lashes are at least a half-inch long – I'm not exaggerating.'

Ursula, however, had no intention of waiting for Bob to make up his mind. When it became obvious to her that he was satisfied with their living together without the prospect of marriage, she sent him back to his mother because her daughter was coming over from Germany. 'How would I explain you living in the same house with us?'

In a huff, Taylor left for Egypt to film *Valley of the Kings* with his former girlfriend, Eleanor Parker. His letters to Ursula were returned unopened. When he returned to Hollywood, Bob called her but she refused to see him. During an interview on the set of *Rogue Cop*, he was asked if his seeing Miss Stanwyck meant anything. 'If you're referring to a recent party,' Bob growled, 'I wasn't with her! I just dropped by for a few minutes and she happened to be there; that's all there was to it.'

'Where is the beautiful Ursula these days,' a reporter asked.

'I don't know,' he said, ending the conversation. 'Furthermore, I don't give a damn!'

But he did. After holding on to an engagement ring for a few weeks, she agreed to see him 'for a few minutes'. Ursula said she played a little game with Bob because they had been dating for two years and that was long enough. If he wasn't going to marry her, she wanted to end the relationship, but on 24 April 1954, Ursula and Bob eloped to Jackson, Wyoming. He made sure the announcement was made the following day and asked Helen to notify Barbara who was shocked, but she sent a congratulatory telegram immediately. The threads of reconciliation she had clung to were finally torn. She was so sure his relationships with Eleanor Parker and Ursula Theiss were passing fancies. In later years, Bob told Purvis that at the time of his marriage to Ursula he still felt a sense of loyalty to Barbara. 'It hurt me to hurt her,' he said. Purvis reminded Bob that he had to pay Stanwyck 15 per cent of his salary. Wasn't that enough?

'I thought she might waive that,' Taylor said. 'I honestly thought she would do that much. She's very wealthy and doesn't need my money.'

But Barbara had no intention of relinquishing this last link to Bob. She refused to talk about his marriage, but repeated, 'There will be no other man in my life.' There were other men in her life, of course, but the love of her life was Robert Taylor. However, what he needed in a woman he found in Ursula, who was twelve years younger. She had suffered in a German labour camp during the war and knew what survival was all about. She was sophisticated enough to know Hollywood was fickle and was not interested in her career as an actress. She was an excellent cook, went on hunting and fishing trips with Bob, did her own shopping and preferred to keep house herself.

While still on their honeymoon in Cloverdale, California, Taylor began filming *Many Rivers To Cross* with Eleanor Parker, who did not know he had gotten married and burst into tears when she heard the news. Bob told Purvis that his marriage was almost over before it began – referring to Eleanor, who was tempting, but not enough for him to stray.

Barbara kept herself busy. 'I have to work. I want to work. I'm an actress and an actress acts.' But the only good script that came along was *Executive Suite* with a cast of great stars: June Allyson, Fredric March, Nina Foch, Walter Pidgeon, Paul Douglas, Shelley Winters, Dean Jagger and William Holden. Barbara's part as the mistress of a dead tycoon was a small but effective one. When June Allyson forgot her lines, Stanwyck was not as patient with her as she had been with Marilyn Monroe. Allyson left the set in tears and made sure she was well prepared the following day.

Executive Suite, directed by Robert Wise, was well received. Nina Foch, who played the tycoon's loyal secretary, suspected Bill Holden and Barbara had been lovers once, but not any longer. 'When I was nominated for an Oscar for Best Supporting Actress,' Foch said, 'Barbara sent me a congratulatory telegram. I thought that was very nice.' Nina lost to Eva Marie Saint in *On The Waterfront*.

Witness to Murder at United Artists was another B thriller and one that kept audiences in their seats. Barbara is the witness and George Sanders was the murderer, but no one believes her. He covers his tracks and spends the rest of the film stalking Barbara and convincing the detective (Gary Merrill) that she's crazy. But Sanders 'gets his' in the end and Stanwyck gets Merrill who, in real life, was married to Bette Davis at the time.

If Barbara was disappointed in her recent films, *Cattle*

Queen of Montana proved that no matter how bad things are, they can get worse. 'Dreadful! Awful!' she cringed. 'You wonder how such a thing could happen. The answer is simply that I made a horrible mistake. One gets taken in by what seems like a good idea, and a sort of rough, temporary screenplay, and you sign to do the picture without ever having seen a completed script.

'Within a week after the start of the shooting, everybody on the set knows that the thing is just not gelling. But by that time, you're hooked. So, you do your best and you hope that nobody goes to see it.'

Barbara plays a cattle baroness in Montana plagued by rustlers and Indians, but Ronald Reagan is there to defend her. 'We filmed in Montana,' he said. 'The lakes up there were only about forty degrees, but Barbara insisted on doing the swimming scene herself instead of using her double, because a realistic close-up of her actual face would be more effective. She was in that icy water a long time and never complained.'

The New York Times said about *Cattle Queen of Montana*, 'Miss Stanwyck manages to hold her own with both the men and the terrain.'

The Blackfoot Indians in Montana 'adopted' Barbara and gave her the name 'Princess Many Victories III' for her braving the elements. In a very impressive ceremony they made her a member of their Brave Dog Society with an equally impressive dedication: 'Princess Many Victories III. She rides. She shoots. She has bathed in waters from our glaciers. She has done very hard work – rare for a white woman. To be a member of our Brave Dog Society is to be known as one of our brave people. Princess Many Victories III is one of us.'

Though Stanwyck deserved this honour, one is reminded of her only camping trip with Taylor. 'Never again,' she vowed. At that time she could not understand his love for guns and horses and the outdoors – all of which she now enjoyed.

Tom Purvis remarked, 'If Barbara made a movie in Montana when she was married to Bob, he would have gone along with her and thrived on it. I don't give a damn what she said about their careers keeping them apart. She made no effort. The unanswered question is why, if she loved him so much. Ursula knew nothing about Bob's hobbies, but she shared them with him and won the guy. Barbara dived in icy waters and learned how to fall off a horse because her heart and soul belonged to acting.'

A year after Ursula and Bob were married, Robert Mitchum and his wife Dorothy hosted a party at Romanoff's in Los Angeles. The Taylors were seated at a table with Lana Turner and her husband Lex Barker when Stanwyck marched through the door with her press agent. Mitchum's wife Dorothy confronted her. 'Do you know who I am?' Barbara hissed. When she refused to leave, Barker stepped in and heard Stanwyck say, 'I came to get a look at Bob and his German whore.' She was ushered out but Bob was humiliated.

The Violent Men, a western at Columbia, released in 1955, is the story of a greedy crippled cattle baron (Edward G. Robinson) driving small landowners from his valley while his wife, played by Barbara, has an affair with his younger brother (Brian Keith). Glenn Ford plays a squatter fighting for his land and the right to marry Robinson's daughter. There are the usual ambushes and cattle stampedes, but not so common is Barbara's stealing her husband's crutches when their ranch is on fire. Robinson survives, Ford gets his land, the girl and top billing in *The Violent Men*. Stanwyck does not survive.

Critics considered the film just another western. *The New*

York Times critic said, 'Mr Robinson is spared destruction because his performance is the best.' However, Mr Robinson said *The Violent Men* clearly established him as a 'has been'.

Escape to Burma with Robert Ryan and released in 1955 was dreadful. Barbara is a plantation owner in Burma and Ryan plays a murder suspect who has a way with elephants. There is no plot, unfortunately. *The New York Times* wrote, 'It says "Escape to Burma". Yet everyone is in Burma or a back lot decked out by industrious "green men" to look like Burma, and how can you escape to a place you're already at? Even the monkeys seem bewildered.'

There's Always Tomorrow, released in 1956, was another loser. Barbara returns to her hometown after many years and reminisces with an old beau, Fred MacMurray, who plays the typical father who is not appreciated by his family and gets caught up in old times with Barbara. Her presence gives the wife and kiddies good reason to have his pipe and slippers waiting when he gets home.

The New York Times critic said, 'For Pete's sake, have mercy on Dad – especially if you are contemplating taking him to see this film.'

With one terrible film after another, the fifties was a frustrating time for Stanwyck. Her name on the billboards still had drawing power, but she was gradually losing out to Elizabeth Taylor, Audrey Hepburn, Susan Hayward, Deborah Kerr, Jennifer Jones, Ingrid Bergman and other dramatic, but more attractive, actresses.

But the worst blow to Barbara's pride was the birth of Taylor's first child, on 18 June 1955. She was on the set of *These Wilder Years* at MGM when the announcement about Bob's newborn son Terry was made on the loudspeaker. Tears swelled in her eyes as she tried to control her emotions. When she could no longer contain herself, she ran to her dressing room and closed the door. One of the cast said, 'We thought Barbara was overjoyed, but when she left in such a state, we all wondered if she was shedding tears of envy, tears of jealousy, or tears of frustration. When she came back to her chair on the set, she was not herself. We were embarrassed because we all cheered at the news and it never occurred to us that Stanwyck would react that way. It was pathetic.'

Barbara had accused Bob of being gay because he wasn't interested in her sexually. She had embarrassed and humiliated him in front of friends, but he was, in reality, a guy who was capable of performing with a woman. Now Taylor had the child he always wanted. In a letter to Tom Purvis he wrote, 'Ursula is going to have a baby and I'm speechless. I never knew a guy could get so excited over something that happens all the time. The best thing I ever did was marrying Ursula!'

For Barbara, all hopes of getting Bob back were dashed . . .

In her search for a quality film, Stanwyck spoke to Harry Cohn at Columbia about playing the beautiful and rich Vera Simpson who falls in love with Frank Sinatra in *Pal Joey*, based on the Broadway musical. The movie was expected to be a blockbuster and though her part would be a small one, it had depth. The socialite, however, had to reek of sexuality, and Cohn did not think Stanwyck was sensual enough. When he could not get Marlene Dietrich, he chose Rita Hayworth, who was ten years younger than Stanwyck. Once again, Barbara had assumed she could play the part of a beautiful, passionate woman and was rejected. Although Dietrich, Cohn's first choice, was closer to 60, she had kept her extraordinary beauty and splendid figure.

'Barbara could envision several aspects of the roles she

wanted,' Helen Ferguson explained. 'Beautiful doesn't have to be gorgeous. Many women exude it without a classic face and that's how Barbara interpreted the parts she wanted. I strongly disagreed with her in regard to Dominique Francon in *The Fountainhead*, I thought she might get away with Vera Simpson in *Pal Joey* because it was her money that attracted men. She didn't have to be beautiful necessarily. Dominique did.

'Vera Simpson was a former showgirl and she did a number called "Zip", a modified striptease. Hayworth could get away with it, but it was not meant for Barbara.'

Shortly after the birth announcement of Taylor's son, Stanwyck fell down a flight of stairs at her home and was rushed to the hospital. X-rays showed that she had suffered a cracked vertebra and torn ligaments. Because she was drinking more than usual, there were rumours that she was drunk at the time. Barbara was a lonely woman at the age of 48. She was still nursing a broken heart. She wondered why Bob had been impotent with her but virile with Ursula, who would probably have more children – children that Barbara couldn't have. Bob loved kids and had wanted to adopt one during their marriage. Instead, she got rid of Dion with a cold handshake and little else.

In *These Wilder Years* Stanwyck plays the director of an adoption agency who is not impressed with James Cagney's eagerness to find his illegitimate son. She tells the court, 'Even an animal feeds its young – and fights and dies for it. I found homes for them, among human beings who didn't just exist for themselves, who gave them names and the love without which nobody grows into somebody with faith and decency.' Unfortunately, Stanwyck could memorise these words, but she couldn't live them.

She had better ideas on how to choose a good film. 'First of all comes the story,' she said. 'It's like building a house. That's your foundation, the basement and the cement. That's solid. That's the important thing. Then your interior decoration is the second thing – that's the director. *That* I want. The third thing is all your decorations. That's my actors. But without the story, it's goodbye. I think the little things will take care of themselves. If your story is good and your direction is good, and the other actors, you have a chance.'

She stooped to *The Maverick Queen* with Barry Sullivan and Scott Brady for Republic Pictures. Barbara plays the title role, of course, described by the theme song that begins, 'I'll tell you a story about the maverick queen, the most dangerous woman in the West.' The film introduced a wide screen process called Naturama, but Republic was noted for its quickie westerns with Gene Autry and Roy Rogers. Though it was not a major studio, Stanwyck said, 'As long as people want to see me, I'll continue to make movies.'

Crime of Passion was another forgettable picture with Sterling Hayden, Fay Wray, Raymond Burr and Virginia Grey, Taylor's former girlfriend, who suffered Barbara's wrath. 'We filmed in 1956,' Virginia said. ' This was five years after I dated Bob and she filed for divorce. I accidentally put my coat on her chair and she tore into me with a vengeance in front of everyone. She never mentioned Bob, but she resented me for going out with him. She had no other reason for hating me.'

In *Crime of Passion*, Barbara kills her husband's boss so he can get a promotion. *The New York Times* commented, 'As for Miss Stanwyck's transition from a nice, sassy gal to a maniacal stalker, we don't believe it, Miss Stanwyck.'

In 1957, Barbara made *Trooper Hook* with Joel McCrea in the title role. It was a good western about a white woman held captive by the Apaches. McCrea rescues her and a half-breed son, but her husband and the community treat her as an outcast. The Indian chieftain wants his son back and during the battle that ensues, Barbara's husband is killed, leaving her free to begin a life with McCrea.

In *Forty Guns* with Barry Sullivan, Barbara is an authoritarian rancher in Arizona with her own posse of hired guns. She had just turned 50, but insisted on doing her own stunts which included being dragged by a horse. She was bruised but unhurt.

In 1958 Robert Taylor cancelled his contract with Metro-Goldwyn-Mayer by mutual consent, 'because I can't save any money on a straight salary'. Between his pension and tax-deferred monies, he left after 24 years with almost a million dollars. He bought a rambling ranch on 110 acres of property in Mandeville Canyon and raised quarter horses. The heavy wood coffee table in the front of the ceiling-high fireplace was the only item he salvaged from the divorce. 'This is my first real home,' he told reporters.

Bob's career was in high gear in the fifties. In 1954 he was voted the most popular male star by the Hollywood Press Association, renamed Golden Globes, that represented 500 million moviegoers in the world. But Taylor was lost without the guidance of his parental studio, as were most of the contract players. Lana Turner said she waited a long time for a limousine to pick her up at a restaurant until it dawned on her that she would have to make these arrangements herself. Taylor admitted he had never made an airline reservation and wasn't sure how to go about it. Maureen O'Sullivan, who played Tarzan's Jane, commented, 'MGM taught us everything except how to cope with life.'

*

After *Forty Guns*, Barbara did not make another film for a period of four years. In an interview for the *San Francisco Chronicle*, she explained her absence very simply. 'Nobody asked me. They don't normally write parts for women my age because America is now a country of youth. We've matured and moved on. The past belongs to the past.'

Film historian David Shipman said, 'Maybe Stanwyck should have stopped working after *Executive Suite* until a good offer came along, but she went on, bossy and managing as ever, in a series of low-budgeters, each more abysmal than the last. She was the only professional thing about most of them.'

Stanwyck was living with her maid Harriet Corey and the ever-faithful Buck Mack. She bought a new house on South Beverly Glen Boulevard that cost $100,000. Her closest friends were Frank Sinatra's ex-wife Nancy, the Jack Bennys, Helen Ferguson and Joan Crawford.

It was 'Uncle Buck' Mack (no relation to Willard Mack) who had been in contact with Dion Fay over the years. Buck urged Barbara to send Dion a wedding gift when he married in the mid-fifties. She paid for a new bedroom set, but arranged everything through Mack. This gesture might have been an indication that Barbara still recognised Dion in some small way, but in 1959 he was arrested for peddling pornographic material and sold a story entitled, 'Does My Mother Hate Me?' to a tabloid. After these incidents, no one dared mention Dion's name in Barbara's presence again. Speaking in general, she said, 'Some kids are born with bad blood just like horses. When a parent has done everything possible, the only solution is to save yourself.'

But *did* Barbara do everything possible? As she had done with Taylor, it was a little gesture too late. Dion said in an interview, 'Sure, I've had my troubles, but they all came after Mother cut me completely out of her life.'

Buck Mack, who had known Barbara as Ruby Stevens, was her only link to the past. His death in 1959 hit her very hard.

There was, however, new life in the Taylor household. On 16 August 1959, Ursula gave birth to a daughter Tessa.

CHAPTER FIFTEEN

The Past Belongs to the Past

Loretta Young was the first movie actress to have her own half-hour weekly TV programme (1953–61). Although she acted in only half the episodes, she introduced all the shows and swept through a doorway in a lavish long gown, with the cameras moving in for a glamorous close-up. At the end, she read a few lines of poetry or a passage from the Bible relating to the programme.

When Loretta was ill on two occasions, Stanwyck substituted for her; she also made four appearances on Dick Powell's *Zane Grey Theater*. Having made the transition from movies to television, Barbara wanted her own weekly show, but did not want it to be a carbon copy of Loretta's. She was eager to do a western. The networks were interested in Miss Barbara Stanwyck, but not riding a horse. They told her that westerns were on their way out.

'On the way out? Not around my house they're not,' she said. 'From six o'clock on it sounds like the last frontier around there. On Mondays it's *Restless Gun* (John Payne) and *Wells*

Fargo (Dale Robertson), Tuesday it's *Cheyenne* (Clint Walker), *Sugarfoot* (Will Hutchins) and *Wyatt Earp* (Hugh O'Brien) and so forth. Do I ever get tired of them? Hell, no. I love it!'

Barbara's idea for her own show was based on James D. Horan's book entitled *Desperate Women*, about courageous women on the western frontier. 'The title of Horan's book is a misnomer,' she explained. 'The women weren't desperate at all. They were just real. Some were good and some were bad. In all the westerns these days – and as I said I love them – the women are always left behind with the kids and the cows while the men do the fighting.

'Nuts to the kids and the cows! There were women who went out and fought, too. That's what I want to do. People say it's not feminine. It isn't! Sure, those women wore guns and britches. But don't kid yourself. They were all females!'

Stanwyck would have to wait seven years for her dream to come true. However, NBC-TV gave her a firm offer, but not a western. They felt she should follow Loretta Young's format. Barbara replied, 'I'm too old and too wealthy to swallow that stuff! I want to play a real frontier woman. I want to go out where the boys go!'

When asked if she was finished as a film star, Barbara replied, 'Sure, why not admit it? I couldn't stay up there forever. It's a man's world and it's getting worse. They aren't writing beautiful adult stories any more. Oh, I know stars who say they can't find anything they want to do in films, but I wouldn't be like that. I just haven't had any offers, period!'

She finally reached an agreement with NBC to do *The Barbara Stanwyck Show*, a weekly series of half-hour episodes, but she demanded complete script approval. And she did not want to emulate Loretta 'because I'm not the type to go swooping in and out of an elegant drawing room in elaborate gowns'.

Stanwyck worked harder at *not* being Loretta than she did at being herself. And though she had done some TV, she did not know the tricks of the trade. Barbara was at the mercy of her directors. During the show's introduction she stood motionless, which made her delivery dull and listless. 'The worst was reading my lines from a teleprompter,' she complained.

The Barbara Stanwyck Show made its debut on Monday, 19 September 1960 at 10.00pm EST. The programme received only mild reviews. Barbara told the press, 'We are prepared to pay top price for our scripts. The foundation of a good show is the story, not the star.' When asked how she felt about Joan Crawford's statement that any movie star who appears on the boob tube is a traitor, Stanwyck sighed, 'For me the reason is simple. I wasn't working in the movies and I wanted to work. What else is there for me to do? I have no hobbies. I suppose that makes me an idiot, but there it is. You're supposed to sculpt or paint or something. I don't, I like to travel, but a woman can't travel alone. It's a bore. And it is a lonesome bore. People say it's very nice that I'm on television. How nice remains to be seen.'

In May 1961, the Television Academy of Arts and Sciences gave her an Emmy award for Outstanding Performance by an Actress for *The Barbara Stanwyck Show*. Two weeks later, NBC cancelled the series. She was angry and complained that the TV networks only wanted action shows and had the theory that women can't do action. 'The fact is I am the best action actress in the world! I can do horse drags and jump off buildings and I have the scars to prove it!'

Robert Taylor was doing very well on television: *The Detectives* ran on ABC-TV for two seasons and, in 1961, moved to NBC, renamed *Robert Taylor's Detectives*. 'I don't own a television set,' he told columnist Hy Gardner who asked Bob why he had succumbed to television. 'It's as simple as ABC,' was the reply. 'A five-letter word: M-O-N-E-Y. If you get the right vehicle, TV is a harmless and lucrative racket. You don't have to worry about rehearsals because there are none. If the series catches on, the episodes can run forever and you can sit back and deposit royalties without ever having to look at yourself on the screen.'

When Taylor's TV show switched to NBC, it was increased to an hour. He was making $300,000 a year plus 40 per cent of the ownership, but the show was cancelled after one season. Fortunately, he was also making movies.

Frank Fay died in September 1961 at the age of sixty-three. Two weeks before his death, he was confined to St John's Hospital in Santa Monica and deemed incompetent. He bequeathed his estate worth $200,000 to Catholic institutions and willed nothing to Dion, who sued and received a small portion after all debts were paid.

Barbara had no comment.

In 1961, after a four-year absence, Barbara was back working in a motion picture with Laurence Harvey, Capucine, Jane Fonda and Anne Baxter in *Walk On the Wild Side*, released in 1962 by Columbia Pictures. The film was based on a novel by Nelson Algren, but lacked all the ingredients of the book. Barbara plays a madam of a New Orleans bordello who takes a shine to a new girl (Capucine), but there is only a hint that Barbara is a lesbian when Laurence Harvey tries to take Capucine away. Columnist Louella Parsons asked Stanwyck, 'I hear you're going to play a madam and a lesbian.' Barbara snapped back, 'I'm shocked! What do you want them to do, hire a real madam and a real lesbian?'

Producer Charles Feldman wanted as much sex in the film

as censors would allow, giving director Edward Dmytryk more problems than already existed. Laurence Harvey, a moody bisexual, resented rewrites that entailed new dialogue every day. He finally stormed off the set and kept everybody waiting for an hour and a half. Barbara let him have it with four-letter words that would make a sailor blush, but she got her point across.

It's difficult to understand why Stanwyck would do a picture about lesbianism since she was very sensitive about the subject. Working on the picture was a mess and so was the finished product. Most critics didn't bother to review *Walk on the Wild Side*, but the few who did were very disappointed. *Variety* said, 'It's obvious that in their treating of prostitution the filmmakers did not want to be offensive to anyone. The result is a somewhat watered-downing of the Nelson Algren story of the Doll House in New Orleans and the madam's affection for one of the girls.

'Laurence Harvey plays a drifter in search of his lady, Capucine. He does it well but not strikingly. Capucine, it turns out, is a member of the Doll House, showing a classic, Garbo-type beauty but somehow limited as to range in emotionality via script and/or direction.

'Barbara Stanwyck is steely as the madam who looks to Capucine for the "affection" she cannot find in her maimed husband.'

The *Austin Chronicle* wrote, 'Tawdry trash, of the finest sort, rife with revolting characters and dreadful performances . . .'

The New York Times was blunt, too. 'It is incredible that anything as foolish would be made in this day and age . . . that it is too strong for the kids is sheer eyewash. It's as naughty as a corn silk cigarette . . . Miss Stanwyck is like something out of moth balls.'

Laurence Harvey said of Stanwyck, 'She was bossy. I never knew which side of the camera she was working on.'

The beautiful Capucine co-starred with Bill Holden in *The Lion* (1962) and *The 7th Dawn* (1964). They had a serious two-year affair and friends thought they might marry, but she was a manic-depressive and had difficulty dealing with life. He did, however, leave her $50,000 in his will. In 1990, at the age of 62, Capucine jumped from the eighth floor of her apartment building in Switzerland.

Barbara returned to television in episodes of *Rawhide, The Untouchables* and *Wagon Train*. In 1961, the Professional Photographers of California named her the First Lady of the Camera. 'I guess they just got to the S's,' she laughed. 'I'll never know how I got it.'

There were rumours that Stanwyck might return to the stage, but she said, 'I would be terrified to face an audience.' It was Taylor who got her to do live radio in front of a small studio audience with him. Eventually she was able to manage that on her own. Helen Ferguson recalled that Barbara did a radio show shortly after her divorce. 'If she didn't have any lines, she went to a dark corner and cried. On cue, she was back at the microphone reading her dialogue beautifully. This took a lot of guts from her because it was a comedy.'

When Barbara was in New York she always had lunch with Joan Crawford who settled on the East coast when she married Pepsi-Cola tycoon, Alfred Steele, and gave up acting. Joan became a widow in 1959 and took her late husband's place on the Pepsi board of directors.

Crawford frequented the exclusive '21' Club for lunch and always sat at the same table on the second floor facing the entrance – to see and be seen. Reporter Shirley Eder tells the story of her and Barbara lunching with Joan who 'dispensed with menus and ordered calves' liver for all three. She chose our vegetable and salad, leaving the choice of dessert to us.'

When Joan left the table to greet a friend, Stanwyck told Eder, 'I hate calves' liver.'

'Why don't you tell her?' Shirley asked.

'I wouldn't dare,' Barbara replied.

When the situation was in reverse and Joan was flying West, her secretary called Stanwyck to arrange a dinner for 5.00pm.

'Who the hell eats dinner so early?' Barbara asked.

'Miss Crawford's stomach will be on Eastern Standard Time,' the secretary explained.

'You tell Miss Crawford that Miss Stanwyck's stomach is on California time,' Barbara said and hung up.

The two women shared a very special friendship, exchanging Christmas and birthday gifts, telephoning and corresponding regularly until Joan's death in 1977. They let their hair down in each other's company while the booze flowed and the ashtrays overflowed.

Crawford had her film rebirth in *Whatever Happened to Baby Jane* with Bette Davis in 1962. Director Robert Aldrich signed the actresses to do another horror picture, *Hush . . . Hush Sweet Charlotte*, in 1964. Joan became ill with a respiratory infection during production and it was doubtful she would return to play the role of Charlotte's evil cousin, Miriam. Aldrich called Barbara, who hesitated as she had done when Joseph Mankiewicz offered her the part of Margo Channing in *All About Eve*. Aldrich needed a quick answer so signed Olivia de Havilland instead to play the plum role of Miriam. Barbara was asked if she wanted to play the old lady sitting on her porch who, it turns out, is the real murderer of Charlotte's fiancé. Barbara turned it down and Oscar winner Mary Astor got the part, and moviegoers loved her. But Barbara had an ace in the hole, and if young moviegoers considered Stanwyck an old-fashioned has-been in 1964, she fooled everyone by doing *Roustabout* with 29-year-old Elvis Presley.

Why? 'I want to be exposed to the younger generation who have probably never heard of me,' she said. 'I had worked with producer Hal Wallis many times so when he called me about a part in an Elvis Presley picture I was naturally curious about the script. I liked it. I played the owner of a broken-down carnival and Elvis is the young roustabout entertainer . . . that kind of thing. I thought working with him would be a lot of fun and it was.'

Roustabout was Presley's sixteenth film and though his movies were not first-rate, they were popular at the box office. Elvis, however, was bored stiff. He preferred a live audience and resented making one mediocre film after another.

Edith Head designed the wardrobes for many of Presley's leading ladies and was very surprised to learn that Barbara was one of them. But there were no glamorous gowns required for *Roustabout*. 'For many years I felt that dungarees should be relegated to the rodeo and the garden,' Edith said. 'Very few women over the age of sixteen had the figure to wear them. But Barbara is one of those women. She looks terrific in a pair of denims, so I had no qualms about putting them on her. She has so much presence that no matter what she wears, she owns the screen. Teaming her with Elvis was a stroke of genius. It gave him credence as an actor and it brought some of the older audiences who would never have watched a Presley film otherwise.'

Barbara did not like Elvis and the feeling was mutual. He wanted Mae West to liven things up in an otherwise routine movie, but his manager Tom Parker thought Stanwyck was the better choice. Elvis and Barbara spoke only their lines to each other, but she told reporters, 'He was a fine person. His manners are impeccable. He is on time and he knows his lines. He was a wonderful person to work with.' Elvis had nothing to say about her, but in private he referred to her as 'the biggest closeted dyke in Hollywood'.

The New York Times gave *Roustabout* a good review: 'It has three assets. One is Mr Presley, perfectly cast and perfectly at ease as a knockabout, leathery young derelict who links up with a small-time transient midway. It also has, as the carnival owner, Miss Stanwyck, and where on earth have you been? And while the carnival canvas yields little in the way of dramatic substance, it does cue in on eleven songs.'

Although this was an exciting rebirth for Barbara, she was saddened once again by the death of her brother Byron in 1964. He had been active as an extra in films, thanks to his sister, and on his own ability became director of the Screen Extras Guild. Byron was filming a television commercial when he had a fatal heart attack at the age of 59. He was survived by his wife, Caryl, and son Brian. Stanwyck rarely talked about her family because she felt it was no one's business.

Helen Ferguson, who was getting on in years, faded out of Barbara's life at this time. Helen was from the 'old school' and not adjusting to the new age of Hollywood. Illness forced her to live in a wheelchair and she moved to Palm Springs, but kept in touch with Stanwyck.

Nancy Sinatra Sr had a 'surprise' birthday party for Barbara every year. Once she failed to show up 'because I wasn't invited'. Perhaps she needed the attention or a 'special' invitation because everyone else was there. Or maybe she had too much to drink. This was taken for granted and her friends understood her loneliness. After all, she had a lot to forget and too much to remember. Barbara and Nancy had several things in common.

They were daughters of New York-area working-class parents and had both married popular entertainers who were involved with Ava Gardner, but Frank Sinatra was hopelessly in love with her and fought long and hard to get a divorce. He married Ava in 1951, but it was a stormy marriage that ended in 1957. Nancy managed to bring up three children, Nancy Jr, Frank Jr and Christina by herself and often without her husband's financial support. Barbara had more affection for the Sinatra children than she ever did for Dion.

Stanwyck wasn't dating anyone and wasn't looking. If she needed an escort for a special occasion, such as the Oscars, she called Cesar Romero or Clifton Webb, her two favourite gay friends. Whenever Barbara was asked about her personal life, Taylor's name was mentioned. 'How long am I supposed to carry that damn torch,' she complained. 'I've heard what some people are saying – that I lock myself up in my house, pining away for him. I'm sure no one wants to live alone, but you have to adjust.'

Stanwyck tried to adjust to television and hoped again for a series. She made a pilot of *The Seekers* about the FBI's Missing Persons Bureau, but nothing happened. 'I'm not giving up,' she said. 'I'm ready to work anytime and I'll take any part that comes along. I don't care about the money or the size of the role. All I care about is working.'

Then there was a strange turn of events. Producer-director William Castle called her regarding *The Night Walker* about a woman trapped in a dream so vividly real that her days and nights blend into a nightmare. Robert Bloch, author of Alfred Hitchcock's *Psycho*, wrote the script. Barbara wanted to do the picture and met with Castle who asked her how she felt about Robert Taylor as her leading man. 'I think it's a wonderful idea,' Barbara replied, 'but you'd better ask Mr Taylor how he feels about it. And Mrs Taylor.'

Bob was out of town at the time so his agent, who knew

good films were at a premium in Hollywood, gave a positive reply on behalf of Taylor, who was furious. Trying to compose himself, he asked to see the script. 'I'll have to give this some thought,' he scowled. 'I wasn't prepared for it.'

Taylor was upset for several reasons. He did not appreciate his agent committing him to anything without his consent, and he did not want to work with Barbara. He told Purvis, 'I might have gotten out of it, but then Castle offered me a percentage of the profits, and I couldn't turn my back on that. Anyway, Barbara and I don't have many scenes together.'

'But you're on the same set every day,' Tom said.

But it was too late for Bob to back out. Castle had already notified the press that Barbara Stanwyck and Robert Taylor were co-starring in the film. When asked by the press how he felt about it, he took the gentlemanly approach: 'Who could pass up the opportunity of working with such a wonderfully talented woman?' he said, forcing a smile. Later he commented to friends about working with Barbara, 'It doesn't seem possible I was married to her.'

In *The Night Walker*, Barbara is a woman tortured by nightmares that she cannot distinguish from reality. Taylor takes the part of the attorney who pretends to help her through the dilemma. In reality he is the one trying to drive her to suicide so he can inherit her estate, but they are not romantically involved in the plot.

The New York Times said, 'The whole thing would not be worth reporting if it didn't have Barbara Stanwyck and Robert Taylor. Miss Stanwyck, silver-haired and seasoned, does lend an air of dignity to the otherwise unbelievable woman in this totally unbelievable tale. And Mr Taylor, lean and wrinkled, does at first make the lawyer seem something more than the spurious character he finally turns out to be.'

The *Journal American* wrote, 'William Castle has two old pros enriching the quality of his new eerie suspense thriller. Barbara Stanwyck and Robert Taylor, coming out of semi-retirement from films, are the invaluable assets in this Universal release.'

Taylor said he didn't know he was in semi-retirement and Barbara felt the same way.

Ursula Taylor was frequently on the set of *The Night Walker* and wanted to make friends with Barbara. Bob was relaxed and in a good mood, but told his wife he wanted nothing to do with his ex-wife socially. He told Ursula, 'Do you realise that every cent I'm making from this movie goes to Barbara?'

'But the woman lost most of her friends and has no family,' Ursula said. 'It might be nice to invite her for dinner.'

'I don't want her in my home,' Bob emphasised.

'Why?'

'Because you don't know Barbara the way I do,' he replied.

Ursula never brought up the subject again.

Coming out of a 10-year slump, Stanwyck felt alive again. She had shocked everyone by doing an Elvis Presley movie and then appearing on screen with Robert Taylor. Helen Ferguson said, 'Barbara was in demand again and loving every minute of it. I think it dawned on her when she was asked to do a coffee commercial. The money was very good, but Barbara turned it down. They kept offering her more money, but she wasn't interested until they threw in a new kitchen, too. Barbara didn't need the money or the kitchen, but agreed to do the commercial. I think it got to the point that she was too embarrassed to turn it down again if they wanted her *that* much.'

CHAPTER SIXTEEN

Victoria Barkley

Stanwyck did not immediately jump when ABC-TV agreed she should play Victoria Barkley in *The Big Valley*, a weekly series of one-hour episodes. As excited as she was, the big question remained: 'What kind of a dame is the widow Barkley?' She refused to sign until her character was established. 'I'm a tough old broad. I do not want to play someone who tiptoes down the staircase in crinoline and wants to know where the cattle went. This is not me!'

Victoria Barkley, therefore, was a stunning woman with class, wit, patience and guts who rode a horse like the wind and handled her buggy like a lady. She could shoot a gun with one hand and pour tea with the other. Victoria wore britches and she wore velvet. She ran the sprawling Barkley spread in California's San Joaquin Valley with a strong hand and the help of her three sons, Jarrod (Richard Long), Nick (Peter Breck), and her late husband's illegitimate son, Heath (Lee Majors). Audra (Linda Evans) was her only daughter. Charles Briles played another son, Eugene, during the first season, but was drafted into the service and did not return to *The Big Valley*.

Each episode was filmed in six days, averaging twelve pages of screenplay a day. Doing movies was easy compared to television. Barbara was up at 4am and worked until nine at night. 'We did twenty-six shows in twenty-six weeks,' she said. 'Twenty-six very fast movies, and no one counts the hours. The script is here, the cameras are there and you are here. Late afternoons you feel you're so hot and tired – especially on those hot locations – and that you just can't do a thing. But somehow you always do. At night you have a pot of soup and go to sleep. It's a brutal life.'

But Stanwyck loved every minute of it! Nothing else mattered except *The Big Valley*. During the three months hiatus when she was not filming, she was bored and restless.

When Stanwyck began the series she had to contend with a young cast of actors who were more concerned about their make-up and costumes than remembering their lines. 'They were always running to their make-up tables,' she complained. 'That's the most important part of their performance – their hairdos! After that, their make-up and their wardrobe and lastly their performance.' Barbara was unhappy with Linda Evans, who was frequently late and unprepared, but the young actress soon learned how to conduct herself. During rehearsal Barbara said, 'You need more presence. I'll show you how in the next scene.' Linda waited and was about to make her entrance when Stanwyck booted her in the butt and exclaimed, 'That's presence!'

'She was the greatest teacher,' Evans said.

Barbara was 60 and couldn't have cared less. 'There is no age in my life that I want to be again,' she said in an interview. 'Certainly not thirty. I have yet to understand the percentage, the advantage, the rhyme and reason, the necessity and/or compulsion to be never older. Maybe I'm just too lazy – it seems much more practical to me to eat properly and to be too busy to be facialed, massaged, chin-strapped, and all the other time-consuming pampering age-fearing ladies submit to – not to mention hair dyes, facelifts, and the expense. At least the samples of the nice, youth-impelled, but I think, misguided ladies I've seen have made me think all the fretting, fussing, stewing, lying and dying, all the tensions created by wanting to be forever young, age one faster. They look what they are – battle-scarred veterans of their lost war against time. I decided not to enlist in that war three years before I turned forty.'

But to keep working in Hollywood, both men and women needed some cosmetic surgery. Male actors had wrinkles removed from around the eyes. Taylor was one of them and he had no vanity. It wasn't a matter of looking younger, but looking more presentable.

Barbara had another advantage. She was thin by nature so there was no need for dieting. She preferred juice and coffee for breakfast, a light lunch and a small steak and side order of peas for dinner.

Critics were not impressed with *The Big Valley* when it aired for the first time on Wednesday 15 September 1965 from 10 to 11pm. Stanwyck wasn't concerned. 'By the time the bad reviews appear in print, the viewer has seen the show already. And he's just as liable to be defensive about the rap, figuring, "The show wasn't as bad as all that!" In the end, it is the viewers themselves who decide whether a show is good or not. They don't need any help to make up their minds. Bad reviews don't hurt me at all.'

The reviews, however, angered Barbara when they compared *The Big Valley* to *Bonanza* (NBC) and Victoria Barkley to Ben Cartwright, 'Our family is much stronger!' she insisted. 'My sons are strong. They are real men. This is not one of those mother-knows-best-things! Hell, I wouldn't play one!

Our family behaves like any normal family. We fight, argue, discuss things. We're not like some of the TV families today. I don't know where the hell these people are. I never see any of these people in real life. The woman I'm playing has plenty of battles with her boys. She's a very vital person. So are her sons. They have minds of their own.'

Stanwyck's sarcasm was aimed at *Bonanza*'s Ben Cartwright and his sons, Adam, Hoss and Little Jo. She was furious when rumour persisted that *The Big Valley* was ABC's version of NBC's top-rated *Bonanza*.

'I guess you have to be compared to something,' she hissed. Then she took a jab at Ben Cartwright played by Lorne Greene, referring to him as 'the Loretta Young of the West'. 'That's not for me!' she spouted.

Stanwyck had gone a little too far this time. *Bonanza* was the number-one television show in the country, and many viewers wrote letters of protest. Later she clarified. 'I have been quoted as saying that I thought Lorne Greene was "the Loretta Young of the Western soap operas". I think I have been misquoted. What I did mean was that I felt he was too pontifical. When he passes judgment – that's that! When Lorne Greene has an opinion, it has to be right. Well, damn it all. I've had my own ranches. I am a horsewoman. I ran ranches and herds and bred livestock years before Lorne Greene even knew what a saddle looked like! And you don't run ranches anywhere by being pontifical about any bit of it. Nobody on my ranch can ever tell what's going to happen next. You can't afford to be too opinionated or too conceited. If you do, you portray the West badly, and you do the West an injustice. The West was rough, hell-country, full of fights and wrongs and hardness. Pontifical wiseacres did not survive long out there!'

One viewer wanted to know when Stanwyck had bred cattle.

Perhaps Barbara's nasty remarks had to do with the fact that *The Big Valley* was never in the top-ten rated television shows. *Bonanza* and *Gunsmoke* were the only westerns to make the list.

Stanwyck refused to stop talking about *Bonanza*. When Dan Blocker, who played the beloved Hoss, complained about his salary, Barbara hit the roof. 'What so-called artist is this who feels he is wasting his talent for $10,000 a week? He seems to feel the public loves him for himself as an actor. But what was he before playing Hoss? The love the public has given him is due to the role, the script, the actions of the person he is employed to play. If he is not a multimillionaire, as he says he is, what a shame, he should continue to fool the public and to accept the love they give him.' She went on to say that actors are servants of the public. Money and fame are secondary to the true artist. 'And to use such terms as "selling one's self", isn't that an insult to the public that watches and likes the show and pays for it all? I probably won't be able to look at Blocker again, not in any role he plays. I'll probably feel he's just prostituting himself again in playing the next role, any role. But it is a fact that the public loves Hoss and has made Dan Blocker a rich man. It is like spitting at an audience that's standing and applauding. That's how I feel.'

In 1966, however, Barbara won an Emmy for Outstanding Performances by an Actress in a Leading Role in a Dramatic Series. She was nominated again in 1967 and 1968. *Photoplay* magazine gave her their Editors Award, engraved, 'To the Eternal Star whose glamour, talent and professionalism both on and off the screen have thrilled millions of fans throughout the years.' *TV-Radio Mirror*'s Television Critics Poll was unanimous in naming Stanwyck as the Best Dramatic Actress in Television.

Suffering from emphysema and a bad back, Barbara had compassion for those who continued on with their work despite illness. She went to the premiere of *The Subject Was Roses* with

Patricia Neal who had recovered from several strokes. 'You're gorgeous,' Barbara said with a hug.

'Oh,' Neal smiled, 'you finally saw *The Fountainhead*.'

Stanwyck pulled away and said, 'I admire you very much.' She was still bitter over losing the choice role of Dominique Francon that she wanted so desperately in 1949. She was not one to forgive or forget with one exception.

Robert Taylor. He had been struggling with mediocre films, but eventually took over as host and occasional star of *Death Valley Days* when Ronald Reagan left the series to run for Governor of California in 1966. Reagan won and moved to Sacramento, but his first stop when he came to Los Angeles was the Taylor ranch.

The close relationship between Reagan and Taylor had nothing to do with Barbara, who was asked to present the Screen Actors Guild Award to the governor on 21 November 1966. Waiting backstage for her cue, she was confused when she heard Reagan's voice on stage: 'The Screen Actors Guild Award is not presented just for long-time excellence on screen. It should be called, perhaps, an above-and-beyond award, because it is given for outstanding achievement in fostering the finest ideals of the acting profession.

'The individual to be honoured has given of herself in unpublished works of charity and good citizenship. So for performance of our craft, as well as for performance as a citizen, this award is being presented from actors to an actor, and I am very proud to present someone whom so many of us have worked with. We have known her in this profession as truly a professional and an exponent of our art and craft of the best, Barbara Stanwyck.'

Shaken and surprised, she walked on stage with an expression of disbelief on her face. Obviously stunned, she tried to compose herself, but tears of joy and gratitude glistened in her eyes. 'This is the first time I've been kissed by a governor,' she said pausing to gather her thoughts. 'I am very, very proud of this moment. I love our profession very much. I love our people in it. I always have and I always will. And whatever little contribution I can make to the profession, or to anything, for that matter, I am very proud to do so. It is a long road. There are a lot of bumps and rocks in it, but this kind of evens it all out, when an event like this happens in your life. From a very proud and grateful heart, thank you very much.'

Reagan explained to the press afterwards, 'If Barbara suspected she was getting an award we were afraid she might not show up, so we invited her to come down and present the award to me.'

In 1968, Stanwyck was the victim of a stalker who appeared one morning when she opened her front door to get the newspaper. She was still living at 273 South Beverly Glen Boulevard in the house she bought after the divorce. She paid little attention to the man until he jumped up and shouted, 'I'm here, Barbara, baby, I love you!!' She threatened to call the police and he left. But when he returned, Stanwyck had him arrested. Henry Roy Belmert, a transient from Ohio, was held for observation, but California law required a jury trial before anyone could be committed to an institution. Barbara testified that she never knew when he was going to jump up and grab her, but there was no evidence against him other than her accusations, and he was released. Unfortunately, he returned and tried to cut through a screen door. Barbara made a hysterical call to police and Belmert was arrested again, but there was no guarantee that he would be held in custody. Terrified, she sold the house and moved to a one-storey ranch house on Loma Vista Drive in Beverly Hills, part of a newly developed Trousdale Estate, where tight security was enforced.

The Big Valley was cancelled in 1969 due to poor ratings, Stanwyck was hurt and disappointed because the cast and crew were her family. It was a great letdown, but she would face another devastating blow in the same year.

CHAPTER SEVENTEEN

There Will Be No Other Man in My Life

In August 1968 Robert Taylor fell to his knees from a violent coughing spell. He and Ursula had just returned from a house party at Rhonda Fleming's. The next day Ursula insisted he see a doctor.

Waiting for the results of the X-rays, Bob wrote to Tom Purvis, 'I'm sorry I agreed to the tests. Couple of years ago the same thing happened. I've had a spot on my lung since I was a kid, and the damn doctors scared the hell out of me until they said I was fine. I swore I'd never go through that again. A few weeks ago I was a pallbearer at Dennis O'Keefe's funeral. He suffered a slow death from lung cancer after they cut him up. I don't know why a guy can't just die with some kinda respect, but the doctors – well, they don't letcha.

'They suspect pneumonia but, Jesus, if I have lung cancer, no way can I keep it from the producers of *Death Valley Days*. They won't wait to find out if I'm gonna make it or not. They'll have to replace me and I can't afford that. Far as I'm concerned, if they want out, I might as well start diggin'. They're gonna getcha – not that they want to – they're just gonna getcha.'

Bob wrote his letters to Purvis the way he talked, in a casual manner that was so like him, but this was not casual. It was serious and heartbreaking. The 57-year old Taylor had been a chain-smoker all his adult life – the one trait he shared with Barbara.

When doctors confirmed a mass on his right lung, it was Ursula who begged Bob to have an operation.

'I want to think about it,' he said.

'If not for yourself, do it for the children and me,' she said.

'My chances are better without going under the knife. Once they're finished with me, I won't have much time left. If I go about my business the way I am, at least I'll be able to work.'

But Ursula pleaded with Bob and on 8 October a portion of his right lung was removed. An announcement was made to the press that Taylor had Rocky Mountain Fever, and he was discharged from the hospital, but Ursula took him home knowing he had cancer. In November, Bob began a series of cobalt treatments. Cancer was not mentioned, but he knew what was wrong. Two operations followed the major one, and on 3 December 1968, the newspapers printed the truth.

Taylor said it was the 'one John Wayne role nobody wants. It was a tremendous shock of course. When I first went into surgery, I didn't know, but they found tumours in the right lung and that was it. But I've got to face it. I'm putting all my faith in the hands of my doctors.'

On Christmas Day, doctors told Ursula that Bob had only a few months to live.

John Wayne called Bob to tell him, 'When they told me I had lung cancer in 1964, it was like being belted across the gut with a baseball bat. The tumour was the size of a golf ball, but I licked it.' He was cancer free until 1978 when he became seriously ill. He died on 11 June 1979 of lung and stomach cancer.

Dale Robertson, Chad Everett, Robert Stack and Ronald Reagan were regular visitors to the Taylor ranch. Bob was in and out of St John's Hospital nine times during his illness. He had faced the fact that death was imminent and hoped it would be sooner rather than later. Medical bills were piling up and he wasn't working. He worried about money and he worried about Ursula. In February, Bob wrote to Tom and ended the letter with 'take care and food fishin'.' It was Taylor's swan song to his best friend. In March he called Bob Stapler, producer of *Death Valley Days* to tell him formally, 'I'm letting you out of your contract. I doubt that I'll be able to work this year.' Stapler wouldn't hear of it and insisted they go over a script for a forthcoming show. He and his crew put up a good front for Taylor who did a few hours' work and felt better for it. However, Stapler left the ranch in tears.

Early in May, Ursula invited Barbara to visit Bob. According to Taylor's ranch hand and confidant, Art Reeves, it came as a surprise and he disapproved, but it was not his place to say so. When Stanwyck got out of the car on the circular driveway, she appeared drunk, but Art concluded she was most likely sedated. Whether Barbara should have been allowed to be at Bob's bedside is irrelevant. She has to be commended for it. Seeing the man she loved for 33 years wasting away on his deathbed was heart wrenching. If she had chosen not to face this, nobody would have blamed her. This was her first visit to the Taylor ranch, and Art Reeves resented it. 'She didn't belong,' he said.

Stanwyck told Bob that she would waive the 15 per cent of his income, what there was of it. This is what he hoped to achieve by seeing her, and for no other reason.

On 26 May Ursula's 24-year-old son from her first marriage, Michael Thiess, died of a drug overdose. A troubled young man, he had been arrested several times and attempted suicide on at least one occasion. Ursula found his body in a motel and called Art Reeves. After talking to police and answering their questions, she collapsed.

Police listed Michael as a 'struggling actor' who, after a year in prison in Germany for trying to kill his father George Theiss, returned to the United States and five convictions for assault and possession of drugs. Taylor would not allow him on the ranch so there were feelings of regret and relief. Bob insisted on being at home with Ursula after her son's funeral and managed to spend a few days at his beloved ranch before giving up the fight. He was taken back to the hospital and, on Friday 6 June, the press were told that Robert Taylor had lapsed into a coma but not before he whispered to Ronald Reagan, 'Tell Ursula, be happy . . .' On Sunday 8 June, he simply closed his eyes . . .

Part of Barbara died too. Was it possible that she had outlived this beautiful man – the young 'Mr Artique' she was so happy to find out was Mr R.T., her blind date for the evening? The innocent kid from Nebraska who called her every day from England with proposals of marriage and hanging up in a huff only to call back again?

At first Stanwyck was sure she could not bear to attend Bob's funeral. Ursula offered her the courtesy of sitting with the family in the private vestibule hidden from the other mourners. Barbara declined, but two days later she had second thoughts. Her mind drifted back over the years when Bob told her, 'Don't wear black to my funeral.'

Helen Ferguson said, 'Barbara did not want to attract attention. The funerals of Hollywood celebrities always drew a crowd of fans and curious people, making a circus of a solemn occasion. She thought her very presence would cause a disturbance, but then she found out that Ursula wanted a very private service at the Church of the Recessional at Forest Lawn Cemetery in Glendale. That convinced Barbara to pay her last respects to Bob. I thought she should sit in private with the Taylor family, but she said it might upset the children, and that she was mourning Bob's loss like the others. But she had been married to him and that made all the difference.'

Barbara Stanwyck, the professional and dedicated actress who always arrived early on the movie set, was pathetically late for the funeral on 11 June 1969. Everyone else was seated and Ronald Reagan was ready to give the eulogy when she appeared, two men holding her up by both arms. The bright yellow dress in itself was startling, but more shocking was the fact that it was Stanwyck who was being guided down the aisle to a front pew. Art Reeves wondered why she didn't sit in back of the chapel if she was so weak and bereft. It didn't make sense to anyone. She had disrupted Bob's funeral before it began.

Barbara was all right until Reagan broke down halfway through the eulogy. He managed to restrain himself, but she wept uncontrollably for the rest of the service. No one else showed the grief that she openly displayed. Reagan turned from the congregation and looked at the widow and her two children. 'Ursula, there is just one last thing that only you can do for Bob – be happy. That was his last thought to me.'

It was over, but everyone kept their seats until Barbara stood up in a faint and had to be half carried out of the chapel. Purvis said the consensus was that Stanwyck had portrayed the 'other widow' to prove for the last time that she had been a vital part of Bob's life. Getting into her car, she received an invitation to the Taylor ranch from Ursula for 'a drink on Bob' – a Hollywood tradition often described as a 'dignified wake'. It was an occasion to remember the good times and, for those who had never met in the past or might never see each other again, to share fond memories of their departed friend.

While the other guests mingled, Barbara was getting drunk. She also spent time conversing with Ursula's daughter, Manuela Theiss, who was trying to adjust after being arrested several times for drunk driving and being in possession of drugs. She would eventually turn her life around for the better, but when Bob was alive, Manuela presented problems. Apparently she and Barbara got along very well that day.

Everyone was uncomfortable while Stanwyck was at the ranch. That she was drinking didn't help matters, but finally she disappeared and was seen talking to Ursula in front of the house. They walked slowly round and round the circular driveway, Barbara doing most of the talking. She told the widow, 'If there is anything I can do, Ursula – anything, please let me know.'

'We didn't know what the conversation was so we were all concerned,' Purvis recalled. 'Ursula had been through enough. She didn't need Barbara to make matters worse. Later we found out Bob thought it was the decent thing to invite Barbara to the ranch after the funeral because she was not going to collect alimony during his illness. We never found out what they said to each other, but finally we saw Barbara's car disappearing down the dusty driveway to Mandeville Canyon Road and we were all relieved.'

'But a few weeks later,' Reeves explained, 'Ursula came running across the front lawn to us screaming, "Damn! Damn! Damn!" I never heard her swear before. Seems she found out from her business manager that Barbara had billed the Taylor estate for alimony until the day he died. Doctor and hospital bills had eaten up every cent of cash Bob had.

'Ursula was hysterical and became very sick. She threw up

and broke out in hives. Bob's psychologist-friend came right over to the ranch and calmed her down by explaining Barbara's actions. It was her way of possessing Bob to the end. It wasn't the money, but it might have been the principle. Ursula, of course, felt used because she had tried to include Barbara and make her feel wanted.

'Word got around Hollywood fast. It had been a well-guarded secret that Bob was paying alimony. It was a double impact to find out he was paying right up until he drew his last breath.'

Barbara was a favourite in the fan magazines after Taylor's death. The story of their courtship and marriage was interesting reading to the younger generation who could only identify with Stanwyck in *The Big Valley* and Taylor in *Death Valley Days*. One article described Barbara's shrine to Bob in her home. It offered a lurid portrait of her after Taylor's funeral – how she put on the nightgown she had worn on her honeymoon with Taylor; how she hung pictures of him throughout her house and ran his movies over and over; that she wore only the jewellery he had given her. Much of this was true except for the nightgown that would have been in tatters after 30 years. But it was true that Stanwyck built a shrine to him in her home. She kept his love letters and read them over and over again. He was very romantic and innocent when he wrote them, and so impetuous and full of energy and hope that she had had to rein him in.

Helen Ferguson said that Taylor specifically requested that certain items be returned to Barbara after his death, 'There were some photos, a money clip, some jewellery, and a gold cigarette case that she had given to him when he was in the Navy.'

Ursula had these items sent to Stanwyck, who never acknowledged receiving them. But apparently she did because a well-known reporter appeared on the Mike Douglas television talk show wearing a St Christopher's medal that was part of the collection. 'It once belonged to Robert Taylor,' the reporter said. 'His wife Ursula gave it to Barbara Stanwyck after his death. Now it's mine. Wasn't that nice of Miss Stanwyck?'

Mike Douglas replied, 'Yes. And wasn't it gracious of Ursula to part with it?'

Ursula Taylor sold the ranch in 1971 for an undisclosed price. To this day the property is referred to as 'The Robert Taylor Ranch' and is worth between $50 and $65 million. Ursula remarried in1975 and resided in Hawaii until her third husband died of lung cancer thirteen years later. Tessa Taylor, Ursula and Bob's daughter, pursued an acting career and her brother Terry is a successful business executive. When their father's home state of Nebraska dedicated The Robert Taylor Memorial Highway in his honour with a film festival in 1994, Ursula and the children participated.

CHAPTER EIGHTEEN

Back to Work

If Barbara thought cigarettes caused Taylor's lung cancer, it didn't stop her continuing to chain-smoke, despite suffering from emphysema that often had her gasping for breath. In the confines of her home, she also continued her heavy drinking to ease the pain of remembering.

Ronald Reagan's eulogy had brought back so many memories of Bob that touched her soul. 'Twenty-four years with one studio, MGM alone . . . His face instantly recognisable in every corner of the world . . . Now there are those in our midst who worked very hard to bring him down with the label "Pretty Boy" . . . His quiet and disciplined manner had a steadying effect on every company he was ever in . . . I know that some night on the late, late show I'm going to see him resplendent in white tie and tails at Delmonico's, and I'm sure I'll smile at Robert Spangler Arlington Brugh Taylor because I'll remember how a fellow named Bob really preferred blue jeans and boots . . . In a little while the hurt will be gone. Time will do that for you. Then you will find you can bring out your memories. You can look at them – take comfort from their warmth.'

Barbara told friends, 'I want to forget the past but the future in Hollywood looks bleak.' The Golden Era was no more. Though she had not been under a long-term contract to any one studio, she understood the security it gave stars such as Taylor, Greta Garbo, Clark Gable and Joan Crawford. 'There were merits,' she admitted. 'Two or three pictures a year written for them by top writers. It was like a baby being bathed and all wrapped up in a blanket. Today, it's catcher catch can. Today somebody buys a book or a play and asks what bank will finance it instead of who should be cast in the film. Today, it's about investments, not personalities. It's about money not about beautiful people in beautiful stories.'

Barbara could afford to complain because she didn't need the money. If she never worked another day in her life, it didn't matter financially. But she needed to keep busy for her sanity. 'I'm tomorrow's women,' she said.

But the tomorrows in Hollywood were fearful ones following the Charles Manson murders on 8 August 1969, two months after Taylor's death. The friendly community of celebrities who thought nothing of leaving their doors unlocked or taking a late-night stroll alone, was in a panic. Actress Sharon Tate who was married to director Roman Polanski and eight months pregnant was among the five people brutally killed for fun, and the word PIG written on the door in Sharon's blood. The following day the Manson's gang murdered Leno and Rosemary Lablanca, ate dinner in their victims' house, took a shower and left. These were senseless slaughters that rocked Hollywood and changed it forever.

Television had taken its toll on Hollywood and changed it

forever, too. Actors were spending more time in New York City to earn a living. Joan Crawford's visits to California were infrequent, much to Barbara's disappointment. She missed her close friend and frequent escort, Clifton Webb, who died of a heart attack in 1966 at the age of 77. The talented star of *Laura* was a well-known homosexual who lived with his mother, whom he adored. His friend Noël Coward commented, 'It must be difficult to be an orphan at seventy.' It was. Webb never got over her death and lived as a recluse for his final years.

Barbara's other gay escort, Cesar Romero, was available, but dreaded hearing from her. 'I wonder what she has planned for me now,' he'd laugh. Cesar was popular as the Latin lover in musicals and as Jane Wyman's love interest in *Falcon Crest*. His career was revived 1966 when he played The Joker in *Batman*.

In 1970 Stanwyck starred in ABC's Movie of the Week, *The House That Wouldn't Die*, produced by Aaron Spelling, who would become television's most successful producer, responsible for *Dynasty*, *The Love Boat* and *Fantasy Island*. In *The House That Wouldn't Die*, Barbara was splendid as a woman living in a haunted mansion in Amish country, and at the age of 63 she was on the set earlier than anyone else and insisted on doing her own stunts, as usual. Her stand-in said, 'Miss Stanwyck was one actress who requested a stunt girl because it provided us with work. Most actors use stand-ins for long shots or when the photographer is lighting the set. Miss Stanwyck did not like to sit still. She stood on her feet when the lighting director was setting up. This is a very tiring and boring procedure, but she was a perfectionist. She asked for a stunt girl but not always use her.'

In 1971 Aaron Spelling asked Barbara to work for him again in *A Taste of Evil*, another ABC Movie of the Week with Barbara Parkins and Roddy McDowell. Stanwyck portrays Parkins' mother, who tries to have her committed to an institution so that she can collect an inheritance she feels is rightfully hers. *A Taste of Evil* was a genuine Stanwyck vehicle: a tough-woman role typical of those that had made her popular in the forties.

In November 1971 Barbara began filming *Fitzgerald and Pride*, a pilot for a potential television series about a woman lawyer and her young partner, played by James Stacy. Her old friend Lee J. Cobb, who had co-starred with her in *Golden Boy*, was to be cast in the series as well. But the project was a jinx for all concerned.

On the second day of filming, Barbara wasn't feeling well but she got through the day. When she suffered stabbing pains on her left side in the middle of the night, she called Nancy Sinatra, who took her to the St John's Hospital in Santa Monica, where both Frank Fay and Robert Taylor had died. Barbara was diagnosed with a ruptured kidney and rushed into surgery, where it was removed. Afterwards, she told friends, 'For two days I was on the other side. It's cold there and very dark. Thank God I came back. Plenty of people survive with one kidney. I'll be fine.'

Stanwyck was replaced in *Fitzgerald and Pride*, renamed *Heat of Anger*, by Susan Hayward who said, 'No actress likes to get a great part this way. I've never met Miss Stanwyck, but it's a hell of a job trying to fit into her shoes.' She sent Barbara three-dozen pink roses with a card, 'From one Brooklyn broad to another'.

Hayward, who was 10 years younger than Stanwyck, won an Academy Award for Best Actress in 1959 for her role in *I Want to Live*. She was diagnosed with brain cancer in 1972 and died two years later at the age 55. At her funeral in Atlanta there was a floral piece with a card – 'From one Brooklyn broad to another'.

In 1973 the *Heat of Anger* jinx hit again when the talented and popular 37-year-old James Stacy lost his left arm and leg in a motorcycle accident.

In January 1973 Barbara felt strong enough to film another Spelling Movie of the Week for ABC. *The Letters* consisted of three mini-stories: John Forsythe in the first, Barbara in the second and Ida Lupino in the third. The plots dealt with letters lost in a plane crash and delivered a year later. The movie did not get good reviews, but the critics praised Stanwyck and Lupino. If Barbara's fans expected to see a sickly star still recuperating from a serious operation, they were delightfully surprised. She had never looked better, and there was a different air about her. After facing death and adjusting to a slower pace, Stanwyck had reached new depths in her acting. She had had a soul-searching experience that brought her closer to God. For once in her life, she had to give in to the expertise and perfection of others: her doctors and nurses.

On 28 April 1973, a radiant and proud Barbara Stanwyck was inducted into the Hall of Fame of Great Western performers in the Museum of the National Cowboy Hall of Fame. The candlelit black-tie ceremony was held in Oklahoma City, and it was her former co-star, Joel McCrea, who gave her the Wrangler Award. Memories were all around her that night. Robert Taylor had been given the same award posthumously in 1970 – the only non-living trustee of the museum. Ursula accepted the award with her son Terry at her side. Taylor had said if he could live in another time and place, it would have been the old West. Stanwyck echoed his feelings.

Barbara said the night she received the Wrangler Award was one of the most rewarding in her career. She described the film clips shown later in the evening. 'It started out in the forties when I was young and it went bang, bang, bang – very fast with still photos and a man narrating. Then it moved into the actual film clips. Whoever edited this did a sensational job because when they started shooting the stunts, it looked as if I were breaking my ass and my neck. The people oohed and aahed. It was quite stirring.'

Barbara was finally receiving the awards and honours so long overdue, but the gruelling 14-hour days were over. Doing nothing was never her favourite pastime, but she was learning to relax and enjoy her accomplishments and reflecting. She said her greatest mistake in life was not returning to the Broadway stage when she was still married to Frank Fay. She put the blame partly on trying to hold her marriage to Bob together, but if she had it to do all over again, Barbara would have found a way to continue her career in the legitimate theatre. 'I wouldn't lie about the offers I've had,' she said regrettably. 'It's so sad because I'd do it if only I had the courage. The fear of facing a live audience in a play is so overwhelming that it seems almost impossible that I was once so unafraid.'

Was her marriage the only reason she did not return to the stage?

'No,' she sighed. 'I fell in love with films. That's a pretty strong reason, isn't it?'

In 1977, Helen Ferguson died in March and two months later Joan Crawford passed away, a victim of pancreatic cancer, in her New York apartment. Barbara did not comment on the loss of her dear friend but a year later, Joan's adopted daughter, Christina, published the damning book *Mommie Dearest* that almost shattered Crawford's sterling image and Barbara was furious. 'Kids are ungrateful and they show it by setting out to destroy their parents,' she said angrily.

Stanwyck had not been seen on television in four years

except in movie reruns and the syndicated *The Big Valley*, but the 71-year old actress looked at least a decade younger when she attended the Academy Awards on 3 April 1978. Wearing a rhinestone-studded black gown and looking slimmer than most of the younger actresses, Stanwyck was asked to present one of the awards.

Master of Ceremonies Bob Hope said, 'There's a lot of gold being given out tonight, but Hollywood will never run out of it as long as we have treasures like the next two stars. He made his sensational screen debut in *Golden Boy*, and we'll never forget his leading lady whose performances are never less than twenty-four karat. The Golden Boy and his Golden Girl are together again tonight. William Holden and Barbara Stanwyck.'

Holden, who was fighting a losing battle with alcohol, would be dead in three years. As he stood next to Barbara, who was 11 years younger, Holden looked haggard and worn out. She outshone him without trying. They adored each other – one reason he decided not to follow the script that night. 'Before Barbara and I present the next award, I'd like to say something. Thirty-nine years ago this month, we were working on a film together called *Golden Boy*. It wasn't going well and I was going to be replaced. But due to this lovely human being and her interest and understanding and her professional integrity and her encouragement and, above all, her generosity, I'm here tonight.'

Barbara was overwhelmed by the applause. With tears filling her eyes, she tried to talk, but all that came out was, 'Oh, Bill!' Then they embraced and she cried for a moment before taking a deep breath and reading the nominations. There was a slight hesitation as she handed him the envelope and said, 'Here, Golden Boy, you read it.'

But there were a few thorns among the roses at this time.

Homosexual author Boze Hadleigh was interviewing famous stars for his forthcoming books about lesbians in Hollywood. Through a mutual friend, Hadleigh managed to get an interview with Barbara in her home. To get started, he showed her a copy of the *Hollywood Star* newspaper with the names of bisexual actresses. She was number one on the list. He pointed out that Joan Crawford was included because her daughter wrote about Joan's lesbian tendencies in *Mommie Dearest*.

Barbara commented, 'It would have killed Joan to be called a lesbian by that daughter of hers. Fortunately, for Joan, that was overlooked in publicity about her being an alleged child beater. That she wouldn't have minded as much as the other.'

'But that's ridiculous. One is hurting a person – a child – the other is pleasuring a consenting adult.'

'I'm talking about Joan, not me. Let's get it over with. What questions?'

Hadleigh asked, 'Do you think bisexuality was very widespread among female stars during Hollywood's heyday?'

'I heard Dietrich, Greta Garbo, most of the girls from Europe swing either way. Then I found out it's true.'

'You found out?'

Stanwyck snapped back. 'Next!'

Hadleigh asked if there was any pressure to marry Robert Taylor. Barbara stood up and snarled, 'Don't you ask me if it was an arranged marriage. I'm damned tired of that impertinent question, Now, please leave.'

Hadleigh apologised, but Stanwyck shouted, 'Get out!'

'Or if the truth bothers you I will take the headline and the list with me – thank you. At least you got top billing – thank you for your time.'

This entire taped interview is in Boze Hadleigh's book, *Hollywood Lesbians* (Barricade Books, 1996).

The fact that Stanwyck's name topped the lesbian list didn't bother her as much as the question about whether her marriage to Taylor was arranged; this she found offensive.

The successful Broadway play *On Golden Pond*, about a couple married for 50 years, was going to be made into a movie in 1981, and Barbara wanted to play Henry Fonda's wife. However, his daughter Jane, who was producing the film, opted for Katharine Hepburn, who won her fourth Oscar as best actress. Henry Fonda was voted best actor but was too ill to accept his award. He died on 12 August 1982.

To prove she was still alive, Stanwyck turned to television once again and made a guest appearance on *Charlie's Angels* that led to a possible series, *Tony's Boys*, with Stanwyck playing Tony, but the idea was shelved.

In 1981 the Film Society of Lincoln Center in New York City wanted to pay tribute to Barbara. She thought it was a nice thought, but her reply was, 'We'll see.' Friends hounded her until she gave in.

'I could understand if they picked Katharine Hepburn,' she told film critic Rex Reed, 'but of course she wouldn't do it. But when they asked me, I thought at first it was a mistake. I thought they got me mixed up with Bette Davis. Attention embarrasses me. I do not like to be on display. I was always an extrovert in my work, but when it comes time to be myself, I'll take a powder every time. I never got an Oscar. I never had an acting lesson. Life was my only training. Eighty-five movies, yes, but that wasn't eighty-five great movies, honey. There were some real clinkers in there. Oh, Lord, yes.'

On 13 April 1981, Barbara Stanwyck arrived at Avery Fisher Hall with her Golden Boy, William Holden. Looking every bit the star, she wore a silver sequin gown and white stole, brilliant complements to her beautiful white hair.

Henry Fonda was too ill to be there, but he sent a telegram: 'Dear Barbara: Can't be at your marvellous evening because I'm having hospital tests. I'm feeling fine, but my only sadness is not being able to be with you at the Film Society of Lincoln Center tribute. Shirley approves of my forty-year love for you, Barbara, and she and I will be honoring you in California. We send our very special love.'

President Ronald Reagan sent a telegram ending with, 'Long before it was fashionable, you were a paradigm of independence and self-direction for women all over the world.'

Walter Matthau commented on Stanwyck's film career: 'She played five gun molls, two burlesque queens, half a dozen adulteresses and twice as many murderers. When she was good, she was very, very good. When she was bad, she was terrific.'

Following a standing ovation, Barbara gave a brief speech: 'When the Film Society first notified me about this stunt, I thought they made a mistake. I thought they meant Barbra Streisand. Well, I got that straightened out. And then I thought I had to tell them that I never won an Academy Award, so we got that straightened out, too. They said that didn't make any difference to them.' Barbara thanked everyone who had helped and guided her throughout the years. She appreciated being chosen for the tribute, which she described as 'a beautiful memory'.

Being seen around Hollywood and New York with William Holden was another rebirth for Barbara. For several years he had been in the public eye romancing actress Stefanie Powers who was co-starring with Robert Wagner in *Hart to Hart*, a popular television series. Despite the 24-year difference in their ages, Bill and Stefanie were very much in love, but his alcoholism posed a threat to their getting married.

It was during a lull in their relationship that Holden and Stanwyck attended a small dinner party given by Nancy Sinatra in the fall of 1981. The other guests said Barbara was listening intently to Bill's complaint about the lack of good scripts in Hollywood, but he thought at last he had found one – *That Championship Season*. Holden was anxious to start filming, but after many delays the outlook seemed dim. 'Of course he always talked about Africa,' one of the guests said, 'and told us he would retire there. But Bill didn't look happy. Stefanie had put the affair on hold until he stopped drinking, but she kept in touch with him.'

Holden took Stanwyck home that night and it was the last time she would see him.

A few weeks later, on 27 October, Barbara was awakened during the night by a masked burglar. 'He was wearing a ski mask,' she said, 'and he had a gun. He wanted to know where I hid my money and jewellery. I was terrified so I told him. I tried to turn on the bedside lamp but he shouted, "I told you not to look or I'll kill you!" and then he hit me over the head with the gun and pushed me into a closet. Blood was running down my face, but somehow I managed to put my hand against the sliding door so it wasn't shut tight. He told me if I tried to get out he'd kill me.'

The thief was over six feet tall and weighed about 200 pounds. 'I was dizzy,' Barbara said, 'and on the verge of passing out, but I was determined not to bleed to death in the closet. Thank God I was able to think straight and put my thumb in the door. I waited and waited. My blood was staining the carpet in the closet and I was losing consciousness, but I had to hang on. When I was positive he was gone, I called the police.' She was taken to Cedars-Sinai Medical Center, treated and released.

The burglar, who cut the glass in a living-room window to

gain entrance, had taken jewellery worth only $5,000 and a cigarette box that Taylor had given her. A neighbour said, 'We were all very surprised that a robbery with such violence should occur in Trousdale Estates. We've never been bothered before. It was a horrible experience for her, being roughed up and having a flashlight in her eyes. He didn't have to pistol-whip a frail seventy-four-year-old lady. Even though her head wound required only a few stitches, Miss Stanwyck told me she would never be the same again – that she was devastated over losing a gold and platinum cigarette box and other pieces of jewellery from Robert Taylor that she treasured so much.'

Before Barbara was beaten and robbed, she had begun a new social life and loved it. She told her neighbour, 'I never had time to relax. My whole life was my career. Then I got sick and almost died. After that things changed.' Stanwyck went on to say how wonderful it was shopping for gowns and shoes and getting her furs out of storage. Old friends asked her out for dinner and she became more enthused over invitations to Hollywood banquets and award dinners.

Barbara had reversed the star system by basking in the spotlight *after* proving her talent as an actress – that is, until the robbery. She paid $10,000 to have an electronic security system installed and locked herself inside the house. When she found out the thief had an accomplice that night, she feared they might come back. After this, Stanwyck rarely ventured out socially unless someone met her at the front door and saw her home.

Already nervous and distraught, Barbara nearly collapsed when she received a phone call on 16 November to tell her that William Holden had been found dead in his Shoreham Towers apartment. With a blood alcohol level of .22 he had apparently tripped over a rug and fallen into the sharp edge of the bedside table, causing a deep cut on his forehead that resulted in him bleeding to death. His apartment manager, who hadn't seen Bill in three days, let himself in and found the body. The Golden Boy was cremated and his ashes scattered in the Pacific Ocean. There was no funeral.

Holden had become a managing partner in an animal preserve country club in Kenya and left this legacy to Stefanie Powers, who used it to create the William Holden Wildlife Foundation.

Two weeks later another former lover of Stanwyck's met with disaster. Robert Wagner's wife, Natalie Wood, drowned on 29 November. While sailing on his yacht off Catalina Island with their friend Christopher Walken, she disappeared during the night, supposedly while trying to get into a dinghy. Her body washed ashore the next morning, and the circumstances of her death have never been fully determined. Bob and Natalie had divorced in 1962, and remarried in 1972.

Stefanie Powers and Robert Wagner, who were co-starring in *Hart to Hart* consoled each other professionally. There was never a hint of romance, but the coincidence of their tragedies was felt around the world.

On 2 February 1982, Stanwyck was rushed to hospital with pneumonia and suffering from an enlarged liver. For three days she was in the intensive care unit in St John's Hospital, but three days later she was much improved and moved to a private room. She told reporters on the telephone, 'They treated me with antibiotics. I've made the turnaround in my recovery. Now I want to work again.'

Producer David Wolper wanted to know if she was serious. If so, was she interested in the role of Mary Carson in his TV miniseries, *The Thorn Birds*? Barbara had read Colleen McCullough's best-selling novel and couldn't wait to get her teeth into the part of the bitchy Carson who tries to seduce her priest.

Unfortunately, the TV script had taken the nastiness out of Mary Carson, and Stanwyck was furious. She called producers Wolper and Margulies using a vocabulary that made their ears sizzle. They reviewed the script and decided she was right and began revisions.

Still recuperating from her bout with pneumonia, Barbara was anxious to regain her strength not only to do *The Thorn Birds*, but to accept a special Oscar from the Academy of Motion Picture Arts and Sciences on 29 March1982.

A young John Travolta introduced her at the ceremonies:

Four years ago William Holden and Barbara Stanwyck came up on this stage to present an award. When they did, Mr Holden departed from the script to speak from his heart. He said that his career derived from the lady standing next to him. All he was came from her generosity, her support, and her abiding belief in him. Barbara was completely surprised by this. She listened, her public face letting her private face show, but just for an instant. The actress in control, and that's the very essence of Barbara Stanwyck's eminence and that hold she has on the audience. She's reality. She's professional and, when she walks across the screen, it's beauty and confidence. She's always the woman she plays and yet she's always herself.

The theatre lights were turned down as film clips from some of Stanwyck's most notable films were shown. The audience was in tears when they watched poor Stella Dallas dressed in rags, peering through a window to catch a glimpse of her daughter being married in a society wedding – and then the policeman telling Stella to 'move along'.

The house lights went up and John Travolta looked to the wings: 'Ladies and gentlemen, Miss Barbara Stanwyck!'

Wearing a clinging, sequined fire-engine-red gown, she walked on stage to a standing ovation. She strode in front of the audience with her famous panther stride with a calm expression on her face as she grasped the microphone and drank in the applause. Finally a hush came over the audience.

Thank you. Thank you very much. I'd like to thank the Board of Governors of the Academy for giving me this special award. I tried many times to get it, but I didn't make it. So this is indeed very special to me. You don't get it alone. There are writers, directors, producers – all their kindnesses to me through the many years. And the people backstage. The remarkable crews that we have the privilege of working with. The electricians, the property men, the stagehands . . . oh, camera . . . they're just marvellous. And my wonderful, wonderful group, the stunt men and the women who taught me so well. I'm grateful to them and I thank them very much.

A few years ago I stood on this stage with William Holden, as a presenter. I loved him very much and I miss him. He always wished that I would get an Oscar, and so tonight, my Golden Boy, you got your wish.

CHAPTER NINETEEN

The Thorn Birds

In June 1982 Stanwyck began filming *The Thorn Birds*. Colleen McCullough's best-selling novel tells the story of a priest who is torn between his love for a woman and his love for God.

Stanwyck imposed her authority on the first day of filming by telling director Daryl Duke, 'I do four takes. That's all.' This was fair warning to the young actors who might not be well prepared, but this would not be the case.

Although Barbara was 75, the make-up people had to put special plastic on her face to make her look older. The younger actresses wanted to know her beauty secrets. 'I've always stayed out of the sun,' she said. 'I eat the right foods and get plenty of rest.'

The Thorn Birds was filmed in the Simi Valley, California, where Mary Carson's prosperous Australian sheep ranch Drogheda was re-created. The spread was not far from Northridge where Barbara and Bob had lived on their adjoining ranches in the late thirties. The cast of players included Richard Chamberlain as Father Ralph de Bricassart, Richard Kiley as

Paddy Cleary, Rachel Ward as Mary Carson's niece, Meggie, the object of the priest's affection, Jean Simmons as Fee Cleary and Christopher Plummer as the archbishop. Interiors were filmed at the Burbank Studio in Los Angeles for the ten hour long episodes of the TV miniseries, with a budget of around $20 million.

The Thorn Birds traced the story of the Cleary clan and their only daughter Meggie after Paddy Cleary moves his family from New Zealand to Australia to help run Drogheda, owned by his wealthy sister Mary Carson. Father Ralph, a frequent visitor at Drogheda, takes an interest in Meggie who is ignored by her family. Mary Carson has a burning passion for the priest and does not take kindly to this. When Meggie blossoms into womanhood, her love for Father de Bricassart is apparent as he struggles to control his for her.

Who can forget the hunger in Mary's eyes when she sees her priest on the veranda after a torrential rain? She watches him undress until he is naked so that he can change into dry clothes. She approaches him and remarks that he is the most beautiful man she has ever seen. She continues to taunts him with questions about how many women have loved him. He asks if that included his mother because even she hated him for loving God more. Mary tells him that even if she is beyond the age of desire, she still has it. As she looks up at him, she strokes his chest as if ready to reach out and kiss him. At this point, Barbara fluffed her lines.

'What the hell,' she exclaimed. 'It's the first time in twenty years I've had a naked man in my arms.'

Barbara's last scene as Mary is her confession but not in the sanctuary of the Catholic Church, but at the entrance to her bedroom as she says good night to her beloved priest. She demands that he kiss her and he tries to kiss her on her forehead, but she demands that he kiss her on the lips, like a man. When he refuses, she exclaims with anger, 'Let me tell you something, Cardinal de Bricassart, about old age and about that God of yours – that vengeful God who ruins our bodies and leaves us with only enough wit for regret. Inside this stupid body I am still young. I still feel. I still want. I still dream and I still love you. Oh, God, how much!'

The next morning Mary Carson is found dead, apparently having taken her own life.

Though Stanwyck won an Emmy for her portrayal of Mary Carson, it was the subject matter of *The Thorn Birds* that got all the attention – a priest breaking his vows of celibacy. It was a shock to many viewers that ABC chose to broadcast the programme on Palm Sunday, 28 March 1983, and running through Holy Week. The third episode, in which Meggie and Father Ralph consummate their relationship, was at the time the fourth highest rated show, preceded only by the final episode of *MASH*, the 'Who Shot JR' episode of *Dallas* and the eighth episode of *Roots*.

In many ways, Stanwyck and Mary Carson were alike. They both loved one man until the day he died, and they got revenge for this unrequited love.

Barbara was in the hospital four times while working on *The Thorn Birds*. Her lifetime of smoking was taking its toll on her health, as did the house-burning scene in *The Thorn Birds*. The smoke was thicker than expected and she inhaled too much of it. She worked until the end of the day before going to the hospital where she stayed for three weeks to take breathing exercises with a deep-breath inhaler. She was put on medication and released. 'It's nothing,' she told reporters. 'The smoke aggravated a respiratory problem I've had for a long time.'

Jean Simmons and Richard Kiley were Emmy winners for Best Supporting Players in *The Thorn Birds*. Golden Globe honours went to the miniseries, Richard Chamberlain, Richard Kiley and Stanwyck, who gave one of the best performances of her career. She attended the award ceremonies and gave a brief 'thank you' speech, but off stage Barbara was unable to catch her breath and was relieved to get into a wheelchair. Doctors warned her to take better care of herself, to avoid damp weather and crowds. A simple head cold could prove fatal. Hospital equipment was set up in her home in case of emergencies.

Stanwyck granted few interviews because 'I've had my time and it was lovely. What am I going to talk about? The golden years are gone. Those who clung to them will face a brick wall. I live alone and doubt I could ever live with anyone again – too dull, some people might say.'

At the age of 78, Barbara was in fairly good health except for her chronic respiratory ailments and a troublesome back. She seemed content to see old friends Jane Wyman, Loretta Young and Nancy Sinatra occasionally, but shied away from the formal limelight.

On the afternoon of 21 June 1985, a motorist driving through the exclusive Trousdale Estates noticed smoke pouring out of Stanwyck's $3 million mansion. She was alone at the time, heard the frantic pounding on her front door and saw neighbours running towards her house. Wearing an old sweater and slacks, Barbara rushed outside just as six fire engines and 55 fire fighters arrived. Only then did she notice the smoke and flames coming from the attic.

'Miss Stanwyck appeared to be in control,' the fire chief said, 'and then she darted toward the house. My men caught her just in time.' Barbara tried to break away and when she realised it was no use, began to sob, 'I must go back inside. You don't understand.'

As the smoke was getting thicker and she was led away from

the house, a neighbour tried to reason with her. 'What's more important than your life, Barbara? The Oscar? Your paintings? What?'

'No, no,' she cried. 'Letters . . . letters and pictures of Bob and me. I have to save them!'

The neighbour said Stanwyck was more concerned about those mementoes than the house. 'It was tragic seeing her standing in the street watching those memories going up in flames if, in fact, they did. The firemen managed to save her valuable paintings, artwork and special awards. I didn't have the heart to ask Barbara about the letters from Robert Taylor and pictures of them together.'

The estimated damage to the house was well over a million dollars. Luckily, some photos and letters were salvaged.

Before the fire, Stanwyck had been in the news regarding the possibility of her signing a contract with ABC Television to play Constance Colby Patterson in *Dynasty II: The Colbys* with Charlton Heston, Ricardo Montalban and Stephanie Beacham. 'I can't think about that right now,' she said. 'The fire has gutted my home and it will take time to make it livable.'

The press reported that it was unlikely Stanwyck would do a weekly television series. A recent cataract operation had left her feeling weak, but reliable sources insisted she was keen on working again.

Dynasty was the top-rated TV series about a wealthy Denver family in the oil business: Blake Carrington (John Forsythe) the patriarch, Krystal (Linda Evans) his former secretary and wife, and Alexis (Joan Collins) his conniving former wife. Most of the show features the conflict between two large corporations, Blake's Denver Carrington and Alexis's ColbyCo.

He played Moses in *The Ten Commandments*, but he has a bad memory. He still thinks he can part the Red Sea.'

Heston referred to Barbara as a 'great broad' and claimed he turned down running for the Senate when she agreed to do *The Colbys*. He was joking, of course, because Heston would never give up acting for anybody. And there was no love lost between him and Stanwyck. She tended to put him down with her innuendos and this led to a clash of egos because Heston was not known for his sense of humour.

The producers suggested a boyfriend on the show for Stanwyck and she said that was fine, 'but I don't want to kiss some old thing with a pot belly.' Friend Joseph Campanella said he'd gladly play her love interest. 'She had a great wit,' he said. 'As we were finishing our first love scene and I said, "You're a mystery lady," the director called, "Cut!" but Barbara didn't stop. She looked up at me and sighed, "God, hold me! Nobody has said that to me in years!"'

But make no mistake. Barbara Stanwyck did not expect to star in a silly soap opera. She wanted some depth and meaning to her character and sensible dialogue. As a seasoned professional, she should have known better. 'This is awful!' she blurted out one day on the set. Another time she exclaimed, 'God, this is boring!'

When Rock Hudson died of AIDS not long after his guest appearance on *Dynasty*, Stanwyck hissed, 'Even if he had been healthy, the scripts would have done him in!' Her comment was not amusing. Except for her beautiful wardrobe, she complained about everything. She flatly refused to wait for any actor who wasn't on the set on time to film. If she was ready, everyone should be ready and Barbara made this very clear. This annoyed those who needed more time for make-up and proper costume fittings. Many of the younger players thought she was too strict.

Stanwyck was asked to play Constance 'Conny' Colby Patterson, sister of Jason Colby played by Charlton Heston. Each episode cost approximately $1 million, but *The Colbys* could hardly be considered in the same league as *Dynasty*. The characters interchanged, however, making it more interesting.

Barbara was offered close to a million dollars for doing 13 episodes as Constance Colby, despite her demands before signing a contract: she would not work more than two days a week, never after six o'clock and not the week before Christmas. She also refused to fall off a horse. 'If you don't like it,' she told producer Aaron Spelling, 'get yourself another girl.'

If Stanwyck thought she no longer yielded power in Hollywood, she was mistaken. Spelling agreed to her terms and she signed the contract. In November 1985 she surprised everyone by attending a party for the casts of *Dynasty* and *The Colbys* held at the Beverly Wilshire Hotel. Those who thought her appearance at the festivities meant she was going to give the new series all the support she could, were sadly mistaken.

Arriving very late, Barbara looked elegant in a black cut-velvet-on-chiffon dress that set off her shocking white hair and youthful ivory complexion. Designer Nolan Miller created the gown and escorted her to the party, but when he introduced to a reporter who wanted to do a story about her, she reacted sarcastically, 'With or without my help I'm sure.'

A glass of champagne mellowed her mood as she watched Linda Evans mingling with the other guests. Stanwyck said that Linda had come a long way since *The Big Valley*. Without showing any emotion she recalled, 'Linda used to giggle a lot. She still calls me "Mom," you know.'

How did she like working on *The Colbys*?

'When I have a problem,' she replied, 'I call for "Moses". That's Charlton Heston, of course. He takes care of everything.

If they were not ready on the minute, she gave them hell. Heston admitted he went out of his way to be prompt because 'Barbara is no Little Miss Sunshine on the set. "She's a great broad," he said. "To say she's a great lady isn't the same thing. She's a great broad in the classic sense of the word. Most actresses would be infuriated by being called a broad. Not Barbara. She comes from an era when men like Gary Cooper and Clark Gable thought being a broad was the best possible thing for a woman to be.'

John Forsythe admitted, 'I've been in this business forty years, but I was very nervous the day I had my first scene with Barbara, but she told me a few bad jokes and put me at ease.'

If it wasn't for the money, why did Stanwyck accept the role of matriarch Constance Colby on a night time soap opera? Because she was happier when she was working and giving herself a chance to be appreciated by another generation. Though Heston's wife Sable, played by Stephanie Beacham, is the bitch in the Colby family, it is Constance who stands up to her. Without spunk and courage, Barbara wasn't interested in the role.

Nolan Miller, who designed Stanwyck's clothes for *The Colbys*, said she made her appearances colourful and she enjoyed it though fashion wasn't her first priority and never was. It was her performance that mattered. She was not on the set at five o'clock in the morning to impress anyone. She began and ended her day with a determined will to give her very best. It was action, not clothes, that made the actress, she stressed, but she went along with the 'Alexis' trend of extravagant clothes to look the part of the wealthy socialite. Wearing a lavender jewelled gown on the introductory credits, Barbara looked stunning.

The Colbys won the Peoples Choice Award in March 1986 for best new show. On stage, the cast stood behind Heston as he gave his acceptance speech. Stanwyck did not attend. It would be humiliating for her to be part of a group accepting an award. She stood alone. *The Colbys* got off to a slow start in the ratings, but made a remarkable comeback. Many critics liked The Colby family better than the Carringtons in *Dynasty*. Thanks to good writing and a popular cast, the show was renewed for another year, but ABC could not get a commitment from Stanwyck, who was quoted by the press as saying, 'This is the biggest pile of garbage I ever did. It's lucky I signed on for only thirteen episodes.'

When the script called for Barbara to be ill, she told the producers, 'I'm not lying in bed with a stupid ailment of an old lady.' As a result, it was arranged for her rival Sable Colby to accidentally back her car into Constance, who would fall to the pavement and suffer a mild concussion. Stanwyck was the boss and she decided for herself what she wanted to be, what she wanted to do, what she was going to say, and how she was going to say it.

Instead of helping the younger players, Barbara was furious and overbearing if anyone did not know their lines or failed to be prompt. It was, however, Stanwyck who was unprofessional, throwing tantrums, telling reporters the show was a turkey, throwing her script on the floor and storming off the set. Those who admired her soon lost all respect for the actress who demanded to be billed as Miss Barbara Stanwyck. A leading player on *The Colbys* who did not want to be identified, said, 'Barbara should have discussed her problems behind closed doors in a dignified manner. She can collect her million dollars, but there are many actors who depend on the show for a living. We were all trying very hard to make it work. It's a soap opera. She knew that when she signed on, but instead of encouragement, she bitched about everything.'

In April 1986 Stanwyck announced she was not returning to

The Colbys. She wanted to stay home, work in her garden and spend time with friends.

And so Constance Colby was killed off in a plane crash, presumably on a trip around the world. Her death was mentioned in the second season, but she did not appear in any of the episodes.

Barbara was not the type to pick up a hoe or plant flower seeds even when she was in the best of health. She couldn't knit, paint, sew or make a pot roast because, very simply, she had no desire to do anything but perform. She was too old to have sex though, like Mary Carson, she still had the desire. Old age had made this talented and cherished actress a frustrated, restless and bitter woman. Often she gasped for breath, but continued to smoke heavily. When she signed to do *The Colbys*, Barbara was barely able to stand up without excruciating pain. Yet she agreed to do it and took great pleasure in denouncing the show and her co-stars. Each day she came to work as if ready to strike, watching the other players with a look of a lioness stalking her prey. In many ways she was a masochist, inflicting pain on herself and those in her path.

Stanwyck was determined to accept all the awards offered to her. She never forgot being snubbed out of an Oscar. She never got over it. She was weak and tired but agreed to attend the American Film Institute black-tie dinner on 9 April 1987 to accept the Lifetime Achievement Award. Though she was in the hospital after spraining her back, she checked out briefly only hours before the telecast and arrived backstage in a wheelchair where she remained until it was time to accept her award.

Master of Ceremonies Jane Fonda said, 'I only made one movie with Barbara Stanwyck. My father was in love with her all his life. He openly admitted it to all his wives.' Testimonials were given from the audience as one by one they stood at their tables. Walter Matthau said Stanwyck knew how to wrap both a good girl and a bad girl into one performance. Fred MacMurray said Barbara was a wonderful girl to work with. 'Once I sent her to jail, once I shot her, once I left her for another woman and once I sent her over a waterfall.' Richard Chamberlain called Stanwyck's raw voice 'a million dollar case of laryngitis'.

When it was time for her to collect the award, Barbara got out of her wheelchair and walked on stage to a standing ovation. It was evident she was in pain as she leaned on the glass podium basking in the applause. 'Honest to God,' she said, 'I can't walk on water.' It was as if she were giving her own eulogy when she told the audience that she owed her career to directors Frank Capra and Billy Wilder. She paid tribute to the crews and other actors and to the all-important writers. There was no emotion in her brief speech. She was matter-of-fact and almost anxious to get it over with. Barbara picked up her award and walked slowly off stage to her wheelchair and oxygen tank.

Stanwyck was not bowing out gracefully. Approaching her eightieth birthday, she told friends it would be nice to work again. She did not want to end her career on a sour note with *The Colbys*, but the deed was done and nothing could change that. She was disappointed. She should have retired with honours after *The Thorn Birds*, but Stanwyck didn't know when to call it quits. She had won every award bestowed on an actress, but with Barbara it wasn't so much the honours, as it was working to attain them.

Dion tried to get in touch with her, but when Barbara refused to talk to him, he sold his story to a tabloid and it was not in her favour. Maybe he didn't turn out as she had hoped, but did Barbara give him a chance? She considered him as 'an unfortunate situation'. Was she referring to the fact that he was an innocent victim of two people trying to save a bad marriage? Dion was used as a Band-aid, unfortunately, but was it his fault that he couldn't heal the break-up of Barbara and Frank Fay? If they hadn't used him, Dion might have been adopted by loving parents and had a better life.

As far as Barbara was concerned, he no longer existed. He had granted interviews and spoke freely about her in 1984, begging her to see him. 'She hasn't been well,' he remarked, 'and I think it's time to make peace.' He said Barbara was disappointed in him because he hadn't turned out to be special. 'I was fat, had freckles all over my face and wore glasses. I was awkward too.' Dion went on to say his father Frank Fay was a heavy drinker. 'He used to beat my mother. They had brutal arguments.' Dion admitted he made mistakes and gotten into trouble but he blamed this on lack of love and attention, a way of fighting back, but for the last twenty years he had been a model citizen and wanted forgiveness.

But true to form, Barbara Stanwyck had no comment.

She had turned back only once – to Robert Taylor after his highly publicised affair in Rome. She had forgiven him and was willing to try again. She was not embarrassed to admit her feelings for him regardless of his affairs.

As for Dion Fay, the reunion with his mother never took place . . .

On 21 June 1988, Stanwyck was taken to St John's Hospital in a private ambulance. She was treated for ten fractured vertebrae in her brittle back. Barbara finally had to face the realisation that she was an invalid. She told the nurse, 'I never thought I would end up like this.' The newspapers reported that she was fighting for her life in the intensive unit, but three weeks later, Barbara returned home. Before she left the hospital she asked for some champagne to celebrate but that was denied her because she was on medication. She had always had faith in her ability to bounce back with enough strength to keep going, but those days were now over and Barbara became a recluse.

Robert Wagner wrote in his memoirs that he spoke to her on the telephone and hoped to visit her, but Barbara wanted him to remember her as she was.

Confined to bed, she surrounded herself with pictures of her and Robert Taylor. Photos of them were everywhere in the room. Nearby was her Oscar that, she believed, was a link to Taylor. 'When I hold it,' she said, 'I'm young again and I can feel his presence. He comes to me in the early hours of each morning. He looks young and handsome just like when I first met him. I wasn't frightened when he first appeared. I was tossing in my sleep. I turned on the light and the Oscar was gleaming on the table. I picked it up and felt an electric shock and then I saw Bob and I knew he was there to guide me to the other side.'

Heavily medicated, Stanwyck was most likely dreaming or delirious, but these illusions gave her peace during these final days.

On 9 January 1990, Barbara was admitted to St John's Hospital again and 11 days later went into a coma. On the afternoon of 20 January, she died in her sleep.

Barbara Stanwyck asked to be cremated and her ashes scattered over Lone Pine, California. There was no funeral.

There is a Hollywood superstition that celebrities die in threes and so it was in 1990. After Stanwyck's death, Ava Gardner succumbed from pneumonia on January 25 at the age of 67. On April 11, Greta Garbo died of kidney failure.

The Films of Barbara Stanwyck

Broadway Nights (First National, 1927)
Producer: Robert Kane
Director: Joseph C. Boyle
Screenplay: Forrest Halsey
Cast: Sam Hardy, Lois Wilson, Louis John Bartels, Philip
   Strange, Barbara Stanwyck

The Locked Door (United Artists, 1930)
Producer: George Fitzmaurice
Director: George Fitzmaurice
Screenplay: C. Gardner Sullivan
Cast: William Boyd, Barbara Stanwyck, Rod La Rocque, Betty
   Bronson, ZaSu Pitts, Henry Snubbs

Mexicali Rose (Columbia, 1930)
Producer: Harry Cohn
Director: Erle C. Kenton
Screenplay: Gladys Lehman

Cast: Sam Hardy, Barbara Stanwyck, William Janney, Arthur Rankin, Louis King

Ladies of Leisure (Columbia, 1930)
Producer: Harry Cohn
Director: Frank Capra
Screenplay: Jo Swerling
Cast: Barbara Stanwyck, Lowell Sherman, Ralph Graves, Marie Provost

Illicit (Warner Brothers, 1931)
Director: Archie Mayo
Screenplay: Harvey Thew
Cast: Barbara Stanwyck, Ricardo Cortez, Charles Butterworth, James Rennie, Joan Blondell

Ten Cents a Dance (Columbia, 1931)
Producer: Harry Cohn
Director: Lionel Barrymore
Screenplay: Jo Swerling
Cast: Barbara Stanwyck, Ricardo Cortez, Sally Blane, Monroe Owsley

Night Nurse (Warner Brothers, 1931)
Director: William A. Wellman
Screenplay: Oliver H.P. Garrett
Cast: Barbara Stanwyck, Joan Blondell, Clark Gable, Charles Winninger, Ben Lyon

The Miracle Woman (Columbia,1931)
Producer: Harry Cohn
Director: Frank Capra

Screenplay: Jo Swerling
Cast: Barbara Stanwyck, Sam Hardy, David Manners, Beryl
  Mercer, Charles Middleton

Forbidden (Columbia, 1932)
Producer: Harry Cohn
Director: Frank Capra
Screenplay: Frank Capra, Jo Swerling
Cast: Barbara Stanwyck, Adolph Menjou, Ralph Bellamy

Shopworn (Columbia, 1932)
Director: Nicholas Grinde
Screenplay: Sarah Y. Mason, Jo Swerling, Robert Riskin
Cast: Barbara Stanwyck, ZaSu Pitts, Regis Toomey, Lucien
  Littlefield

So Big (Warner Brothers, 1932)
Director: William Wellman
Screenplay: J. Grubb Alexander, Robert Lord
Cast: Barbara Stanwyck, George Brent, Guy Kibbee, Bette Davis,
  Dickie Moore, Alan Hale

The Purchase Price (Warner Brothers, 1932)
Director: William Wellman
Screenplay: Robert Lord
Cast: Barbara Stanwyck, George Brent, Lyle Talbot, Hardie
  Albright, David Landau

The Bitter Tea of General Yen (Columbia, 1932)
Producer: Walter Wagner
Director: Frank Capra
Screenplay: Edward Paramore

Cast: Barbara Stanwyck, Nils Asther, Toshia Mori, Walter Connolly

Ladies They Talk About (Warner Brothers, 1933)
Directors: William Keighley, Howard Bretherton
Screenplay: Sidney Sutherland, Brown Holmes
Cast: Barbara Stanwyck, Preston Foster, Lyle Talbot, Lillian Roth

Baby Face (Warner Brothers, 1933)
Director: Alfred E. Green
Screenplay: Gene Markey, Kathryn Scola
Cast: Barbara Stanwyck, George Brent, Donald Cook, Margaret Lindsay, John Wayne

Ever in My Heart (Warner Brothers, 1933)
Director: Archie Mayo
Screenplay: Bertram Milhauser
Cast: Barbara Stanwyck, Ralph Bellamy, Otto Kruger, Ruth Donnelly

Gambling Lady (Warner Brothers, 1934)
Director: Archie Mayo
Screenplay: Ralph Block, Doris Malloy
Cast: Barbara Stanwyck, Joel McCrea, Pat O'Brien, Claire Dodd, C. Aubrey Smith

A Lost Lady (First National, 1934)
Director: Alfred E. Green
Screenplay: Gene Markey, Kathryn Scola
Cast: Barbara Stanwyck, Ricardo Cortez, Frank Morgan, Lyle Talbot, Philip Reed, Hobart Cavanaugh

The Secret Bride (Warner Brothers, 1935)
Director: William Dieterle
Screenplay: Tom Buckingham, F. Hugh Herbert, Mary McCall Jr
Cast: Barbara Stanwyck, Warren William, Glenda Farrell, Grant Mitchell

The Woman in Red (First National, 1935)
Director: Robert Florey
Screenplay: Mary McCall Jr, Peter Milne
Cast: Barbara Stanwyck, Gene Raymond, John Eldredge, Philip Reed, Arthur Treacher

Red Salute (United Artists, 1935)
Producer: Edward Small
Director: Sidney Lanfield
Screenplay: Humphrey Pearson, Manuel Seff
Cast: Barbara Stanwyck, Robert Young, Cliff Edwards

Annie Oakley (RKO, 1935)
Associate Producer: Cliff Reid
Director: George Stevens
Screenplay: Joel Sayre, John Twist
Cast: Barbara Stanwyck, Preston Foster, Melvyn Douglas, Andy Clyde, Clief Thunder Bird

A Message to Garcia (20th Century Fox, 1936)
Producer: Darryl F. Zanuck
Director: George Marshall
Screenplay: W.P. Lipscomb, Gene Fowler
Cast: Wallace Beery, Barbara Stanwyck, John Boles, Alan Hale

The Bride Walks Out (RKO, 1936)
Producer: Edward Small
Director: Leigh Jason
Screenplay: J.P. Wolfson, Philip Epstein
Cast: Barbara Stanwyck, Robert Young, Gene Raymond, Ned
Sparks, Billy Gilbert, Hattie McDaniel

His Brother's Wife (MGM, 1936)
Producer: Lawrence Weingarten
Director: W.S. Van Dyke
Screenplay: Leon Gordon, John Mechan
Cast: Barbara Stanwyck, Robert Taylor, Jean Hersholt

Banjo on My Knee (20th Century Fox, 1936)
Producer: Darryl F. Zanuck
Director: John Cromwell
Cast: Barbara Stanwyck, Joel McCrea, Walter Brennan, Buddy
Ebsen

The Plough and the Stars (RKO, 1937)
Associate Producer: Cliff Reid, Robert Sisk
Director: John Ford
Screenplay: Dudley Nichols
Cast: Barbara Stanwyck, Preston Foster, Barry Fitzgerald, Una
O'Connor, Bonita Granville

Interns Can't Take Money (Paramount, 1937)
Producer: Benjamin Glazer
Director: Alfred Santell
Screenplay: Rian James, Theodore Reeves
Cast: Barbara Stanwyck, Joel McCrea, Lloyd Nolan, Lee
Bowman

This is My Affair (20th Century Fox, 1937)
Producer: Darryl F. Zanuck
Director: William A. Seiter
Screenplay: Allen Rivkin, Lamar Trotti
Cast: Robert Taylor, Barbara Stanwyck, Victor McLaglen, Brian
    Donlevy, Sidney Blackmer, John Carradine

Stella Dallas (United Artists, 1937)
Producer: Samuel Goldwyn
Director: King Vidor
Screenplay: Sarah Y. Mason, Victor Heerman
Cast: Barbara Stanwyck, John Boles, Anne Shirley, Alan Hale,
    Tim Holt

Breakfast for Two (RKO, 1937)
Producer: Edward Kaufman
Director: Alfred Santell
Screenplay: Charles Kaufman, Paul Yawitz, Viola Brothers Shore
Cast: Barbara Stanwyck, Herbert Marshall, Glenda Farrell,
    Donald Meek

Always Goodbye (20th Century Fox, 1938)
Producer: Darryl F. Zanuck
Director: Sidney Lanfield
Screenplay: Kathryn Scola, Edith Skouras
Cast: Barbara Stanwyck, Herbert Marshall, Ian Hunter, Cesar
    Romero, Lynn Bari

The Mad Miss Manton (RKO, 1938)
Producer: Pandro S. Berman
Director: Leigh Jason
Screenplay: Philip G. Epstein

Cast: Barbara Stanwyck, Henry Fonda, Sam Levene, Frances Mercer

Union Pacific (Paramount, 1939)
Producer: Cecil B. DeMille
Director: Cecil B. DeMille
Screenplay: Walter DeLeon, C. Gardner Sullivan, Jesse Lasky Jr
Cast: Barbara Stanwyck, Joel McCrea, Akim Tamiroff, Robert Preston, Brian Donlevy, Anthony Quinn, Evelyn Keyes

Golden Boy (Columbia, 1939)
Producer: William Perlberg
Director: Rouben Mamoulian
Screenplay: Lewis Meltzer, Daniel Taradash, Sarah Y. Mason, Victor Heerman
Cast: Barbara Stanwyck, William Holden, Adolphe Menjou, Lee J. Cobb, Sam Levene

Remember the Night (Paramount, 1940)
Producer: Mitchell Leisen
Director: Mitchell Leisen
Screenplay: Preston Sturges
Cast: Barbara Stanwyck, Fred MacMurray, Beulah Bondi, Sterling Holloway

The Lady Eve (Paramount, 1941)
Producer: Paul Jones
Director: Preston Sturges
Screenplay: Preston Sturges
Cast: Barbara Stanwyck, Henry Fonda, Charles Coburn, Eugene Pallette, William Demarest

Meet John Doe (Warner Brothers/Frank Capra Productions, 1941)
Producer: Frank Capra
Director: Frank Capra
Screenplay: Robert Riskin
Cast: Gary Cooper, Barbara Stanwyck, Edward Arnold, Edward Arnold, Walter Brennan, Spring Byington, James Gleason

You Belong to Me (Columbia, 1941)
Producer: Wesley Ruggles
Director: Wesley Ruggles
Screenplay: Claude Binyon
Cast: Barbara Stanwyck, Henry Fonda, Edgar Buchanan, Ruth Donnelly

Ball of Fire (RKO, 1942)
Producer: Samuel Goldwyn
Director: Howard Hawkes
Screenplay: Charles Brackett, Billy Wilder
Cast: Gary Cooper, Barbara Stanwyck, Oscar Homolka, Tully Marchall, S.Z. Sakall, Dana Andrews, Dan Duryea, Allen Jenkins

The Great Man's Lady (Paramount, 1942)
Producer: William A. Wellman
Director: William A. Wellman
Screenplay: W.L. River
Cast: Barbara Stanwyck, Joel McCrea, Brian Donlevy

The Gay Sisters (Warner Brothers, 1942)
Producer: Henry Blanke
Director: Irving Rapper
Screenplay: Lenore Coffee

Cast: Barbara Stanwyck, George Brent, Geraldine Fitzgerald, Donald Crisp, Gig Young, Gene Lockhart

Lady of Burlesque (United Artists, 1941)
Producer: Hunt Stromberg
Director: William A. Wellman
Screenplay: James Gunn
Cast: Barbara Stanwyck, Michael O'Shea, Iris Adrian

Flesh and Fantasy (Universal, 1943)
Producers: Charles Boyer, Julien Duvivier
Director: Julien Duvivier
Screenplay: Ernest Pascal, Samuel Hoffenstein, Ellis St Joseph
Cast: Edward G. Robinson, Charles Boyer, Barbara Stanwyck, Betty Field, Robert Cummings, Thomas Mitchell, Charles Winninger, Anna Lee, Dame May Whitty, C. Aubrey Smith, Robert Benchley

Double Indemnity (Paramount, 1944)
Producer: Joseph Sistrom
Director: Billy Wilder
Screenplay: Willy Wilder, Raymond Chandler
Cast: Fred MacMurray, Barbara Stanwyck, Edward G. Robinson, Porter Hall, Jean Heather

Hollywood Canteen (Warner Brothers, 1944)
Producer: Alex Gottlieb
Director: Delmer Daves
Screenplay: Delmer Daves
Cast: Joan Leslie, Robert Hutton, Dane Clark, Janis Paige
Guest Appearances: Barbara Stanwyck, Joan Crawford and other Warner Brothers stars

Christmas in Connecticut (Warner Brothers, 1945)
Producer: William Jacobs
Director: Peter Godfrey
Screenplay: Lionel Houser, Adele Commandini
Cast: Barbara Stanwyck, Dennis Morgan, Sydney Greenstreet, Reginald Gardiner, S.Z. Sakall, Una O'Connor

My Reputation (Warner Brothers, 1946)
Producer: Henry Blanke
Director: Curtis Bernhardt
Screenplay: Catherine Turney
Cast: Barbara Stanwyck, George Brent, Warner Anderson, Lucille Watson, Eve Arden

The Bride Wore Boots (Paramount, 1946)
Producer: Seton I. Miller
Director: Irving Pichel
Screenplay: Dwight Mitchell Wiley
Cast: Barbara Stanwyck, Robert Cummings, Diana Lynn, Peggy Wood, Patric Knowles, Robert Benchley, Natalie Wood

The Strange Love of Martha Ivers (Paramount, 1946)
Producer: Hal B. Wallis
Director: Lewis Milestone
Screenplay: Robert Rossen
Cast: Barbara Stanwyck, Van Heflin, Lizabeth Scott, Kirk Douglas, Judith Anderson, Darryl Hickman

California (Paramount, 1947)
Producer: Seton I. Miller
Director: John Farrow
Screenplay: Frank Butler, Theodore Strauss

Cast: Ray Milland, Barbara Stanwyck, Barry Fitzgerald, Albert Dekker, Anthony Quinn

The Two Mrs Carrolls (Warner Brothers, 1947)
Producer: Mark Hellinger
Director: Peter Godfrey
Screenplay: Thomas Job
Cast: Humphrey Bogart, Barbara Stanwyck, Alexis Smith, Nigel Bruce

The Other Love (United Artists, 1947)
Producer: David Lewis
Director: Andre de Toth
Screenplay: Harry Brown, Ladislas Fodor
Cast: Barbara Stanwyck, David Niven, Richard Conte, Gilbert Roland

Cry Wolf (Warner Brothers, 1947)
Producer: Henry Blanke
Director: Peter Godfrey
Screenplay: Catherine Turney
Cast: Errol Flynn, Barbara Stanwyck, Richard Basehart, Geraldine Brooks, Jerome Cowan

Variety Girl (Paramount, 1947)
Producer: Daniel Dare
Director: George Marshall
Screenplay: Edmund Hartmann, Frank Tashlin, Robert Welch, Monte Brice
Cast: Bing Crosby, Bob Hope, Ray Milland, Gary Cooper, Barbara Stanwyck, Alan Ladd, Dorothy Lamour and most of the Paramount players

B.F.'s Daughter (MGM, 1948)
Producer: Edwin H. Knoph
Director: Robert Z. Leonard
Screenplay: Leonard Davis
Cast: Barbara Stanwyck, Charles Coburn, Van Heflin, Keenan Wynn

Sorry, Wrong Number (Paramount, 1948)
Producers: Hal B. Wallis, Anatole Litvak
Director: Anatole Litvak
Screenplay: Lucille Fletcher
Cast: Barbara Stanwyck, Burt Lancaster, Wendell Corey, Ann
Richards, Ed Begley, Leif Erickson

The Lady Gambles (Universal, 1949)
Producer: Michel Kraike
Director: Michael Gordon
Screenplay: Roy Hugging
Cast: Barbara Stanwyck, Robert Preston, Stephen McNally, Leif
Erickson

East Side, West Side (MGM, 1949)
Producer: Voldemar Vetluguin
Director: Mervyn LeRoy
Screenplay: Isobel Lennart
Cast: Barbara Stanwyck, James Mason, Ava Gardner, Van
Heflin, Cyd Charisse, Nancy Davis, William Conrad

The File on Thelma Jordon (Paramount, 1950)
Producer: Hal B. Wallis
Director: Robert Diodmak
Screenplay: Ketti Frings
Cast: Barbara Stanwyck, Wendell Corey, Paul Kelly

No Man of Her Own (Paramount, 1950)
Producer: Richard Maibaum
Director: Mitchell Leisen
Screenplay: Sally Benson, Catherine Turney
Cast: Barbara Stanwyck, John Lund, Phyllis Thaxter, Richard
  Denning, Milbourne Stone

The Furies (Paramount, 1950)
Producer: Hal B. Wallis
Director: Anthony Mann
Screenplay: Charles Schnee
Cast: Barbara Stanwyck, Walter Huston, Wendell Corey,
  Judith Anderson, Beulah Bondi, Gilbert Roland, Albert
  Dekker

To Please a Lady (MGM, 1950)
Producer: Clarence Brown
Director: Clarence Brown
Screenplay: Barre Lyndon, Marge Dekker
Cast: Clark Gable, Barbara Stanwyck, Adophe Menjou

The Man With a Cloak (MGM, 1951)
Producer: Stephen Ames
Director: Fletcher Markle
Screenplay: Frank Fenton
Cast: Joseph Cotton, Barbara Stanwyck, Louis Calhern, Leslie
  Caron, Jim Backus

Clash by Night (RKO, 1952)
Executive Producers: Jerry Wald, Norman Krasna
Producer: Harriet Parsons
Director: Fritz Lang

Screenplay: Alfred Hays
Cast: Barbara Stanwyck, Robert Ryan, Paul Douglas, Marilyn
Monroe

Jeopardy (MGM, 1953)
Producer: Sol Baer Fielding
Director: John Sturges
Screenplay: Mel Dinelli
Cast: Barbara Stanwyck, Barry Sullivan, Ralph Meeker

Titanic (20th Century Fox, 1953)
Producer: Charles Brackett
Director: Jean Negulesco
Screenplay: Charles Brackett, Walter Reisch, Richard Breen
Cast: Clifton Webb, Barbara Stanwyck, Brian Aherne, Robert
Wagner, Thelma Ritter, Audrey Dalton, Richard Basehart

All I Desire (Universal, 1953)
Producer: Ross Hunter
Director: Douglas Sirk
Screenplay: James Gunn, Robert Blees
Cast: Barbara Stanwyck, Richard Carlson, Maureen O'Sullivan,
Richard Long

The Moonlighter (Warner Brothers, 1953)
Producer: Joseph Bernhard
Director: Roy Rowland
Screenplay: Niven Busch
Cast: Barbara Stanwyck, Fred MacMurray, Ward Bond

Blowing Wild (Warner Brothers, 1953)
Producer: Milton Sperling

Director: Hugo Fregonese
Screenplay: Philip Yordan
Cast: Gary Cooper, Barbara Stanwyck, Ward Bond, Ruth Roman, Anthony Quinn

Witness to Murder (United Artists, 1954)
Producer: Chester Erskine
Director: Roy Rowland
Screenplay: Chester Erskine
Cast: Barbara Stanwyck, George Sanders, Gary Merrill

Executive Suite (MGM, 1954)
Producer: John Houseman
Director: Robert Wise
Screenplay: Ernest Lehman
Cast: William Holden, June Allyson, Fredric March, Barbara Stanwyck, Walter Pidgeon, Shelley Winters, Paul Douglas, Louis Calhern, Nina Foch, Dean Jagger

Cattle Queen of Montana (RKO, 1955)
Producer: Benedict Bogeaus
Director: Allan Dwan
Screenplay: Howard Estabrook, Robert Blees
Cast: Barbara Stanwyck, Ronald Reagan, Jack Elam

The Violent Men (Columbia, 1955)
Producer: Lewis J. Rachmil
Director: Rudolph Mate
Screenplay: Harry Kleiner
Cast: Glenn Ford, Barbara Stanwyck, Edward G. Robinson, Dianne Foster, Brian Keith

Escape to Burma (RKO, 1955)
Producer: Benedict Bogeaus
Director: Allan Dwan
Screenplay: Talbot Jennings, Hobart Donavan
Cast: Barbara Stanwyck, David Farrar, Robert Ryan

There's Always Tomorrow (Universal, 1956)
Producer: Ross Hunter
Director: Douglas Sirk
Screenplay: Bernard C. Schoenfeld
Cast: Barbara Stanwyck, Fred MacMurray, Joan Bennett

The Maverick Queen (Republic, 1956)
Associate Producer: Joe Kane
Director: Joe Kane
Screenplay: Kenneth Gamet, DeVallon Scott
Cast: Barbara Stanwyck, Barry Sullivan, Scott Brady, Mary
  Murphy, Wallace Ford, Jim Davis

The Wilder Years (MGM, 1956)
Producer: Jules Schermer
Director: Roy Rowland
Screenplay: Frank Fenton
Cast: James Cagney, Barbara Stanwyck, Walter Pidgeon

Crime of Passion (United Artists, 1957)
Executive Producer: Bob Goldstein
Producer: Herman Cohen
Director: Gerd Oswald
Screenplay: Joe Eisinger
Cast: Barbara Stanwyck, Sterling Hayden, Raymond Burr, Fay
  Wray, Virginia Grey

Trooper Hook (United Artists, 1957)
Producer: Sol Baer Fielding
Director: Charles Marquis Warren
Screenplay: Charles Marquis Warren, David Victor, Herbert
    Little Jr
Cast: Joel McCrea, Barbara Stanwyck, Earl Holliman

Forty Guns (20th Century Fox, 1957)
Producer: Samuel Fuller
Director: Samuel Fuller
Screenplay: Samuel Fuller
Cast: Barbara Stanwyck, Barry Sullivan, Dean Jagger, John
    Ericson, Gene Barry, Robert Dix

Walk on the Wild Side (Columbia, 1962)
Producer: Charles K. Feldman
Director: Edward Dmytryk
Screenplay: John Fante, Edward Morris
Cast: Laurence Harvey, Capucine, Jane Fonda, Anne Baxter,
    Barbara Stanwyck, Donald Barry, Joanna Moore

Roustabout (Paramount, 1964)
Producer: Hal B. Wallis
Director: John Rich
Screenplay: Anthony Lawrence, Allan Weiss
Cast: Elvis Presley, Barbara Stanwyck, Joan Freeman, Leif
    Erickson, Sue Ann Langdon, Pat Buttram

The Night Walker (Universal, 1965)
Producer: William Castle
Director: William Castle
Screenplay: Robert Bloch

Cast: Robert Taylor, Barbara Stanwyck, Hayden Rorke, Judith Meridith, Jess Barker, Lloyd Bochner

The House That Wouldn't Die (ABC Television, 1970)
Producer: Aaron Spelling
Director: John Llewellyn Mosey
Teleplay: Henry Farrell
Cast: Barbara Stanwyck, Richard Egan, Michael Anderson

A Taste of Evil (ABC Television, 1971)
Producer: Aaron Spelling
Director: John Llewellyn Moxey
Teleplay: Jimmy Sangster
Cast: Barbara Stanwyck, Barbara Parkins, Roddy McDowell, William Windom

The Letters (ABC Television, 1973)
Executive Producers: Aaron Spelling, Leonard Goldberg
Producer: Paul Junger Wire
Director: Gene Nelson (Story 2)
Teleplay: Ellis Marcus, Hal Sitowitz
Cast: Story 2 – Barbara Stanwyck, Leslie Nielson, Dina Merrill

The Thorn Birds (ABC Miniseries, 1982)
Executive Producers: David Wolper, Edward Lewis
Producer: Stan Margulies
Director: Daryl Duke
Teleplay: Carmen Fulver, from the novel by Colleen McCullough
Cast: Richard Chamberlain, Rachel Ward, Jean Simmons, Piper Laurie, Richard Kiley, Ken Howard, Christopher Plummer, Barbara Stanwyck

Bibliography

Crane, Cheryl, *Lana: The Memories, the Myths, the Movies*, Running Press, USA, 2008

Fleming, E.J., *The Fixers*, McFarland & Company, Inc. Publishers, North Carolina, USA, 2005

Gardner, Ava, *My Story*, Bantam, New York/London, 1990

Guilaroff, Sidney, *Crowning Glory*, General Publishing Group, USA, 1996

Hadleigh, Boze, *Hollywood Lesbians*, Barricade Books, USA, 1996

Madsen, Axel, *Stanwyck*, HarperCollins Publishers, New York, 1994

Madsen, Axel, *The Sewing Circle*, Robson Books Ltd, 1998

Porter Darwin & Danforth Prince, *Hollywood Babylon*, Blood Moon Productions, Ltd, USA, 2008

Theiss, Ursula, *But I Have Promises to Keep*, Xlibris Corp, USA, 2007

Thomas, Bob, *Joan Crawford*, Simon and Schuster, New York, 1978

Wagner, Robert J., *Pieces of My Heart*, Harper Entertainment, 2008

Wayne, Jane Ellen, *Robert Taylor*, Robson Books Ltd., 1987

Wayne, Jane Ellen, *Stanwyck*, Arbor House, New York, 1987

Index